Frank Lloyd
MASTER OF SCREEN MELODRAMA

ANTHONY SLIDE

Frank Lloyd: Master of Screen Melodrama
© 2009 Anthony Slide. All Rights Reserved.
No part of this book may be reproduced in any form or by any means, electronic, mechanical, digital, photocopying or recording, except for the inclusion in a review, without permission in writing from the publisher.

Published in the USA by:
BearManor Media
P O Box 71426
Albany, Georgia 31708
www.bearmanormedia.com

ISBN 1-59393-472-6

Printed in the United States of America.
Cover Design by Sue Slutzky
Book design by Brian Pearce | Red Jacket Press.

TABLE OF CONTENTS

Acknowledgements 5

Introduction 9

From Actor to Director 17

Adapting Charles Dickens 29

The Sea Hawk *and* The Divine Lady 47

From Silents to Sound 69

Cavalcade *and the British Image* 81

Mutiny on the Bounty *103*

The Paramount Features *117*

The 1940s *133*

A Farewell to the Screen *145*

Bibliography *155*

Appendix A: "Slapped by the Ocean" *161*

Appendix B: "In the Tomorrow of Film Production" *163*

Appendix C: "Hollywood, Get Courageous" *167*

Appendix D: Filmography *171*

Index *187*

ACKNOWLEDGEMENTS

I had thought about writing a study of Frank Lloyd's films for a number of years. I was always intrigued by him and I have been a great admirer of two of his productions in particular, *The Divine Lady* and *Cavalcade*. However, I was always daunted by the length of Lloyd's career and the sheer quantity of his films. There are too great a number to discuss in large detail in a book with any potential for commercial success. As *Photoplay* writer Howard Sharpe put it in 1936, "He has directed so many motion pictures than nobody can remember them all and he himself doesn't want to remember some of them."

Every few months or so, I would return to Frank Lloyd, writing a little bit more and researching a little further into his life and career. Eventually, I decided it was time to finish the book, to concentrate on the director's major contributions to film history, and to publish a relatively slim volume that will, hopefully, serve as an introduction to and a reference work on Frank Lloyd, and encourage others to seek out his films and appreciate just what this extraordinary Hollywood filmmaker had accomplished.

There are a number of institutions and individuals whom I must thank for making this book a reality. Primary research was undertaken at the Margaret Herrick Library of the Academy of Motion Picture Arts and Sciences. At the University of Southern California, I would like to thank Ned Comstock in the Cinema Library, Sandra Lee in the Warner Bros. Archives, and Dace Taub in the Southern California Regional History Center. A number of rare Frank Lloyd films were screened through the courtesy of the UCLA Film and Television Archive.

For personal reminiscences of Frank Lloyd, I am indebted to Ernest Borgnine and Norman Lloyd. Lloyd Hughes' daughter, Isabel Falck, spoke with me in regard to her father's work on *The Sea Hawk*. Frank Lloyd's granddaughter, Antonia Gray Guerrero, provided some useful information. Individuals who offered help include Bob Dickson, Bill Doyle, Robert Gitt, Jere Gulden, and Marty Kearns, as well as the staffs of Larry Edmunds Bookstore and the Samuel French Bookstore. Special thanks to Sue Slutzky.

This book would not have been published had it not been for Ben Ohmart, the amiable owner of BearManor Media. His support and enthusiasm is appreciated beyond words.

The majority of photographic illustrations are from the author's archives; others were provided by the Academy of Motion Picture Arts and Sciences.

Why did I write this book? I can only again quote Howard Sharpe and the concluding words of his 1936 article:

"Frank Lloyd, and the work he does, are both on a grand scale. Than which sentence I can offer no greater evidence of my personal admiration."

INTRODUCTION

Open any book on American film history and examine the index under "Lloyd." Harold will be there, and well represented by multiple page references, and you may perhaps find references to actors Christopher and Norman Lloyd, but where is Frank Lloyd? He does not even make it into Andrew Sarris' 1968 seminal work, *The American Cinema: Directors and Directions 1929-1968*. As far as Sarris and his fellow (and sister) critics are concerned, Frank Lloyd is less important than such marginal figures as Byron Haskin, Charles Walters, Stuart Rosenberg, Hubert Cornfield, or David Miller.

Andrew Sarris is doubly insulting to Lloyd in that not only does he not consider him worthy of an entry, but trashes him in his listing for Cecil B. DeMille, who makes it to what Sarris describes as "The Far Side of Paradise":

"DeMille's cross-reference is Frank Lloyd, and interested or rather disinterested critics might profitably compare DeMille's *Union Pacific* with Lloyd's *Wells Fargo*, or DeMille's *Reap the Wild Wind* with Lloyd's *Rulers of the Sea*, or DeMille's *The Crusades* with Lloyd's *If I Were King*. The comparison in each instance is almost fantastically favorable to DeMille. Where Lloyd's spectacles are dull, heavy and monotonous; DeMille's are well paced and logically constructed."

DeMille's *The Crusades* superior to *If I Were King*? I don't think so. And why does Sarris not compare DeMille's epics with Lloyd's *Cavalcade* or *Mutiny on the Bounty*? *Reap the Wild Wind* is a major DeMille epic, whereas *Rulers of the Sea* is one of its director's lesser works.

There can be little argument that Frank Lloyd is generally not able to claim the label of an "auteur," but, at the same time, there are films for which he does deserve such accreditation. Each of his films is stylistically very different. Neither was he a great innovator, but nor were so many other studio directors of Hollywood's golden age.

Ernest Borgnine, who co-stars in Frank Lloyd's last film, appropriately titled *The Last Command*, described the director simply as "one of best, brilliant to work with; he knew his business; he knew his actors."[1] It is a succinct and realistic summation. Aside from being a prime example of an industry professional, Frank Lloyd is also, arguably, the least appreciated of Hollywood's major directors. He won the Academy Award for Best Direction of *The Divine Lady* in 1929 and of *Cavalcade*, the Best Picture winner in 1933, and he also directed the 1935 Academy Award winner for Best Picture, *Mutiny on the Bounty*, receiving a nomination for Best Direction. Lloyd was the preeminent director of historical drama, be it British (as with *The Sea Hawk*, *The Divine Lady*, *Cavalcade*, or *Mutiny on the Bounty*) or American (as with *Maid of Salem*, *Wells Fargo* and *The Howards of Virginia*.)

Frank Lloyd is the only British-born director to be nominated by the Academy of Motion Picture Arts and Sciences in the 1920s and 1930s. He is the only Scotsman ever to win an Academy Award, and, as a piece of minor Academy trivia, he is one of only two directors (the other was Lewis Milestone for *Two Arabian Knights*) to receive an Academy Award for Best Direction for a film, *The Divine Lady*, that was not nominated in the category of Best Picture.

His career extends from the pioneering days of the silent film, when Lloyd made his debut as an actor in 1913, through the "golden age" of Hollywood in the 1920s, 1930s and 1940s, until his demise as the director of two lesser productions at Republic Pictures in 1954 and 1955. Frank Lloyd began directing in 1914 and worked with some of the biggest names in Hollywood, from Lon Chaney, Jackie Coogan, Clara Bow, Corinne Griffith, Milton Sills, and Richard Dix in the silent era, through Leslie Howard, Clark Gable, Charles Laughton, Ronald Colman, Claudette Colbert, Cary Grant, and Loretta Young, in the 1930s and 1940s. In all, he was responsible, as a director, for more than 125 films.

Frank Lloyd wrote many of his own films in the 1910s, in the 1920s he was active as his own producer, and in the early 1940s, he served as producer of the films of others. He was the consummate Hollywood filmmaker, at ease with the studio system, with the budget, the storyline, the cast and the crew, and yet basically unpretentious about his work. Because he was first and foremost a businessman, working within a business, Frank Lloyd never considered that film should be treated as an art form. It was nothing more than an evening's entertainment, a piece of merchandise, which he produced and which theatre audiences purchased from him. As Lloyd explained his approach in a 1936 interview, the greatest task of filmmaking was not in the actual shooting, but in the preparation: "A good picture...a best-selling picture, must have three basic qualities for success — entertainment value, an important idea or thought, and good characters."[2] His was a sensible procedure, and one adopted by many of today's crop of younger directors, but not one for which he was likely then or later to receive any critical praise. Seldom did Lloyd discuss film as an art form — the artistry was unconscious, undefined and never obtrusive.

His credentials within the community were impeccable: he had helped found the Academy of Motion Picture Arts and Sciences, one of the original officers filing for its charter at its May 1927 launch, and served as its president from October 1934 through October 1935. Lloyd was

Pauline Frederick as Madame X.

on the board of the Screen Directors Guild, and also helped create what became the Motion Picture and Television Fund. In the 1940s, he served as chairman of the Academy Committee overseeing what was to become its Margaret Herrick Library and its film archive. At a time when few had an interest in preserving film history, this director who had no conceit in regard to his own career was anxious that the work of his contemporaries and of Hollywood's pioneers be saved.

Above all, Frank Lloyd understood the "art" or concept of screen melodrama. He could take a hoary theatrical classic melodrama such as *East Lynne*, and transform it into a major film achievement. He brought the novels of Charles Dickens and Victor Hugo to the screen for the first time in feature-length format, and in 1920, Lloyd was responsible for the first major motion picture adaptation of *Madame X*. Based on the 1908 play by Alexandre Bisson, which borrowed elements from *East Lynne*,

Madame X has obvious similarities to *East Lynne*, with which it is comparable as one of the greatest of stage melodramas. Her husband forbids its heroine, Jacqueline Floriot, to see her dangerously ill son after she has been caught in an illicit affair. Jacqueline remains a "lady," despite being reduced to a life in the gutters of Paris, and, twenty years, later is defended in court on a murder charge by her son, now an attorney and unaware of her true identity. The ending is neither happy nor unhappy in that it is a third party who reveals the identity of Madame X to her son, but the reconciliation of the two is very short as Jacqueline quickly dies. The courtroom sequence — the film's climax — is, of course, pure melodrama, and the film also contains classic melodramatic elements of mother love, remorse, dishonor, unfair characterization, deliverance, and self-sacrifice. *Madame X* is very much a woman's picture — one of the first such genuine articles — and as a prime example of this genre adds another type of production to Frank Lloyd's body of work.

The restraints of melodrama on the printed page — and even on the stage — were irrelevant to Frank Lloyd. He could "open up" a melodrama for the big screen, and yet, at the same time, he could control a sweeping saga, such as the original, 1924, version of *The Sea Hawk*, *Cavalcade* or *Mutiny on the Bounty* and capture its finest and most personal melodramatic qualities. Captain Bligh's famous speech concerning Mr. Christian's "hanging from the highest yardarm in the British fleet," delivered as he stands at the prow of the small boat in which he and his supporters have been cast adrift, is unalloyed melodrama at its best. The smallness of the setting, of the boat, against a large and empty sea, in no way negates the sheer power of Charles Laughton's delivery. Here, as elsewhere, the pageantry and splendor that has been seen on screen and is still to come cannot diminish the quiet and intimate moments in a Frank Lloyd production.

In reviews of his historical dramas and of his "smaller" productions, contemporary critics constantly referred to "melodrama" and the "melodramatic." It would appear almost that no Frank Lloyd picture could be described without the use of such terminology.

Melodrama emphasizes the sensational and the emotional elements of the story. It combines the romantic and the realistic. This is never more true than in Charles Dickens' *Oliver Twist*, that Lloyd brought so memorably to the screen in 1922. The Frank Lloyd adaptation bears no similarity to the first U.S. presentation of the novel in play form back in the 1870s, when it was little more than a series of tableaux rather than a full-bodied representation of the novel. The heavy scenery and the equally "heavy" effects of the stage melodrama disappeared with its transition to film. It was Edwin S. Porter who, arguably, first successfully translated stage melodrama to the motion picture with *The Great Train Robbery* in 1903. It was Frank Lloyd who refined and sophisticated it, introducing a successful narrative continuity to match the techniques of the new art form.

In terms of the motion picture, melodrama is a very general (and somewhat vague) description that in more recent years has been broken down into sub-genres and reclassified as everything from *film noir* to horror — two genres missing from a Frank Lloyd filmography, although some might argue that *Blood on the Sun* qualifies as *film noir*. Theorist Siegfried Kracauer wrote of the legitimate ambiguity of the term melodrama.[3] Yet there is nothing ambiguous or arguable about Frank Lloyd's melodramas. They easily fall into that general category be they sea-faring dramas, literary adaptations or studies of contemporary relationships.

Melodrama may be defined as the artificial or the spectacular, but whereas the latter description might often be applied to a Frank Lloyd production, that same work could never be exemplified by the former description. It is the characterizations and their development that always predominate — as in the best melodramas in other media. Frank Lloyd does not reach for special effects or technical virtuosity — although it is certainly present in his films — but rather he is a director who captures the human emotion, the melodramatics of life, through his players. As early as 1919, the trade paper *The Moving Picture World* had noted, "Mr. Lloyd has been especially successful in producing mob scenes of intense realism, and depicting against such backgrounds the most delicate of love stories with strong effects."[4]

Cavalcade contains some of the most spectacular moments put on screen up to that time, and yet a study of its two most memorable sequences illustrates very clearly how its director can allow the grand historical picture to play out in the background while emphasizing the intimate in the foreground. In the magnificent scenes of the departure of the troop ship for the Boer War, it is the emotional farewells of the two families, from above and below stairs, that dominate and even transcend the enormity of the set. As the film winds down to its inevitable conclusion, we watch, along with Diana Wynyard as the grieving mother who has just learned that her son has been killed, as the crowds in London's Trafalgar Square celebrate the Armistice. The focus is on the mother, inconsolable with grief but desperate to be a member of the partying throng, pathetically waving a noise maker in her hand. She is almost lost in the crowd, but not lost to our eyes or our hearts.

Yes, there is an arguable (but amiable) pomposity to Lloyd's direction, but it is there only because the subject matter demands it. The approach must always be sober, strong and forceful.

It is not technical effects or flamboyant direction that predominate, but the storyline. Time and again, Lloyd wrote and spoke of the importance of a good story. As one reporter noted, "He locks himself into a room with script men and adaptors, orders food and beer and cartons of cigarettes, rolls up his sleeves and sets to work. When the door opens a few days later he emerges disheveled and triumphant in a cloud of stale smoke, clutching a battered script complete with dialogue and scenes. A good third of them, in most cases, he has written himself."[5] As early as 1915, Lloyd commented, "The play's the thing. In my mind there is no question about it."[6] It was an opinion from which he never veered throughout his directorial career.

Frank Lloyd left his mark on film, and had little time for discussion of his personal life. "We must keep our private lives out of our business and sell our work on its merits," he wrote in 1925.[7] The lack of anything salacious, real or suspected, in his personal life has obviously played a part in modern disinterest. However, despite an unwillingness to discuss his personal life, it is obvious that Lloyd's background had some influence on his choice of film subject or, perhaps more correctly, those subjects that were chosen for him by studio production heads. He was at his best with British, or more precisely English, themes. But while Lloyd grew up in the Shepherd's Bush area of West London, he was actually born in Cambuslang, a suburb of Glasgow, on February 2, 1886, one of seven children born to an Irish-Welsh mother and an English-Welsh father. Despite his being the most prominent Hollywood filmmaker to be born in Scotland, and after a few beers it was reported that he acquired a discernible Scottish accent, it is obvious that his native land had no influence whatsoever on Lloyd's career. Nor, in any substantial way, have Scotland or the Scottish honored him — their most important contribution to world cinema.

What he did develop at an early age, and what is apparent in several of Lloyd's films, is a love of the sea, resulting from his father's work as an engineer installing turbine engines in ships at ports throughout the United Kingdom. He fondly reminisced that as a child he had walked to Trafalgar Square to view Nelson's Column for the first time, and that experience must surely have influenced Lloyd's version of the love affair between Lord Nelson and Emma Hamilton in *The Divine Lady* (1929). As early as 1913, he was appearing in pirate dramas at Universal, and in 1924, Lloyd directed the most prominent of all silent seafaring melodramas, *The Sea Hawk*. In the 1930s, he directed not only the classic seafaring drama, *Mutiny on the Bounty*, but also the lesser-known *Rulers of the Sea* (1939).

After some minor stage work in London, including fifteen weeks at the Shepherd's Bush Theatre, Frank Lloyd immigrated to Canada in 1909, traveling steerage. A hefty-looking guy, with features that were neither overly attractive nor ugly but suggestive of authority and power, Lloyd had the notion of using his muscle to become a lumberjack. He also considered joining the Royal Canadian Mounted Police. Instead, he took up farm laboring until a chance encounter in Winnipeg with the Walker Theatrical Enterprises, a very minor touring company, encouraged him to return to acting. He made his North American stage debut in Edmonton, Alberta, where he also met his wife, Cincinnatti-born Alma Haller, a German-American soubrette with the Lewis and Lake Company. The couple was married on July 11, 1913.

Frank Lloyd once quoted Henry Arthur Jones that "The theatre is nothing but the place where a man finds himself 'up against' something, and attacks it."[8] It was, however, the motion picture where eventually Lloyd found himself, attacked the new art form and succumbed to it.

As he recalled in the 1950s,

"I had finally found my lasting métier. Delivering green groceries after school — fitting feet with shoes — the singing impersonations — cleaning up after the farm animals — the one-night stands — stringing high wire on the construction gang — chasing burlesque strip-teasers — playing Hollywood heavies — writing by the reel — entertaining in neighborhood movie houses to help pay for the baby — all served as part of the sum total: a director deals in people."[9]

---

1. Ernest Borgnine in an interview with Anthony Slide, August 6, 2002.

2. Quoted in Howard Sharpe, "The Star Creators of Hollywood: Frank Lloyd," p. 101.

3. Siegfried Kracauer, Theory of Film: The Redemption of Physical Reality, p. 215.

4. The Moving Picture World, July 12, 1919, p. 215.

5. Howard Sharpe, The Star Creators of Hollywood: Frank Lloyd," pp. 101-102.

6. "Good Story Absolutely Necessary to Successful Photo Plays, Says Frank Lloyd," p. 15.

7. Frank Lloyd, "Publicity and Exploitation," p. 19.

8. Frank Lloyd, An Outline of the History of Drama, p. 19.

9. With the Tide, p. 61.

CHAPTER ONE

From Actor to Director

As a journeyman actor, Frank Lloyd appeared in playlets on the Pantages vaudeville circuit, traveling as far South as San Diego. He also appeared at the Century Theatre in Los Angeles in 1913, and, following the advice of a fellow actor, applied for and was given work at Universal, performing, initially, in the company's 101 Bison brand, and then moving on to the Rex and Gold Seal brands of films. Unlike most other producers of the period, Universal assigned "brand names" to its films, with groups of players assigned to one brand or the other. Audiences might then know which of its favorite actors or actresses were to be found under a certain brand name and look out for that brand in the program of the neighborhood theatre.[1]

In old age, Lloyd recalled that his first Universal film was directed by Lois Weber and that he appeared as a member of the Royal Canadian Mounted Police.[2] He did not recall the film, but, based upon research, the only production I can locate in which a Canadian Mountie appears, directed by Lois Weber, is the curiously titled two-reel production of *Genesis IV – 9*, released on September 25, 1913. Frank Lloyd's name does not appear in the cast list, but this signifies nothing in that only a few actors are credited in these early productions. A Western drama, the twenty-minute short subject concerns a woman who believes her sweetheart has fallen in love with another woman and so marries his brother.

Lloyd was always to remember the advice he received from Lois Weber:

"Since this was the early silent screen era, Miss Weber urged above all else to concentrate upon the expressiveness of the eyes as an actor's most compelling asset. Her advice still holds true, despite talkies, wide screen and color. The eyes have it."[3]

Extant films of Frank Lloyd as an actor indicate that while no one might doubt his ability, he would never be little more than a screen "heavy." If leads were to come his way, they would be more as a blue-collar worker than a romantic or sophisticated leading man. If he was to leave his mark as an actor, it would be as a villain, not a hero. Lloyd did not possess the virile good looks of such matinee idols of the 1910s as Wallace Reid or Herbert Rawlinson, an actor with whom he worked at Universal, and he certainly lacked the boyish charm of a Robert Harron or a Richard Barthelmess. Heavy-set, both in body and facial expression, he was closer in appearance to William Desmond, William Russell or George Siegmann, none of whom has left much impression as silent leading men.

The range of villainous characters that Lloyd played at Universal range from the gambling title character in *The Temptation of Edwin Swayne* (released on January 14, 1915) and a cattle rustler in *His Captive* (released on April 7, 1915) to William Conway, "a slave to drink," in *Nature's Triumph* (released on April 25, 1915) and the villainous tenement owner Frank Carter in *Through the Flames* (released on August 13, 1914). All manner of ethnic characters came his way. Lloyd was a French Apache leader, who mistreats his woman, played by Grace Cunard, in *The Madonna of the Slums* (released on November 11, 1913), a half-breed, Juan, in *For the Freedom of Cuba* (released on January 24, 1914, and featuring Essie Fay with her trained horse "Arabia"), Pedro, "a questionable character," in *On the Rio Grande* (released on July 5, 1914), and Giuseppi Draga, the leader of an Italian Black Hand gang, in *Circle 17* (released on July 30, 1914). He played South African villains in at least two films: Boer farmer Hans Breitmann, "a brute of a man," in *Dangers of the Veldt* (released on April 11, 1914) and dishonest foreman Landers in *Prowlers of the Wild* (released on July 11, 1914). He even played Scottish roles in at least two productions: Private Ian McGregor, who leaves his native Glasgow for the South African war in *The Law of the Land* (released on February 12, 1914) and Ian MacDouglas in episode three of the 1915 serial, *The Black Box* (released on March 22, 1915).

The last two were sympathetic characterizations, and a number of "hero" roles did in fact come Lloyd's way. He was an Italian hero, Beppo, in *His Last Serenade*, released on March 7, 1915. A week later, on March 15, 1915, theatre audiences saw Lloyd, heavily made-up as the title character, a kindly old man, in *Martin Lowe, Financier*. In truth, as a valued member of the Universal stock company, in more than fifty one- and two-reel productions, released between 1913 and 1915, Lloyd played all manner of roles from William Jones, a sheep herder "with a romantic sentiment," in *The Dead Line* (released on January 7, 1914) to a butler in *The Woman in*

Black (released on June 26, 1914) and a valet in *Traffic in Babies* (released on November 22, 1914). In *A Prince of Bavaria*, released on September 20, 1914, Lloyd was again a valet, but one who changes roles with his master, the title character played by Herbert Rawlinson, on a trip to the United States.[4] A lack of inspiration among Universal screenwriters would often result in Lloyd's playing a character named "Frank."

The most prominent of the films in which Frank Lloyd appeared was the six-reel historical drama, *Damon and Pythias*, starring William Worthington and Herbert Rawlinson in the title roles, under the direction of Otis Turner. Lloyd had the prominent part of Dionysius, "the tyrant of Syracuse," and *The Moving Picture World* (December 12, 1914), described his performance as "conscientious." A somewhat half-hearted commendation. The feature opened at the New York Theatre, New York, on November 23, 1914.

There was never any suggestion by Lloyd or his colleagues that he was a great, or even good, actor. As one commentator noted, "On a rainy afternoon in Hollywood, you can still hear people asking each other who was the worse movie actor, Frank Lloyd or W.S. Van Dyke, and the jury is still out."[5] Lloyd himself would joke that "I was so bad [at acting] that they had to put me on directing in self-defense."[6]

Frank Lloyd was one of a number of future directors — including Jack Conway, Rupert Julian, Robert Z. Leonard, and Marshall Neilan — appearing in Universal one- and two-reel productions in the early 1910s. John Ford was there also, working as a prop man. As already noted, the most prominent of silent women directors, Lois Weber, was active at Universal at this time, but Lloyd worked only briefly with her, spending most of his screen acting career with Otis Turner — and it was Otis Turner who deserves credit for teaching Frank Lloyd the craft of filmmaking. The "Dean of Universal Motion Picture Directors," as he was then described Otis Turner is completely forgotten today, and there are no film classics, major or minor, associated with his name.

Born in Fairfield, Indiana, on November 29, 1862, Otis Turner had been a relatively unimportant theatrical figure (but one who claimed to have been associated in the production of plays for Charles Frohman and Henry W. Savage) before entering the film industry with the Selig Polyscope Company of Chicago circa 1908. For Selig, in 1910, Turner directed *The Wonderful Wizard of Oz*, one of the earliest screen adaptations of L. Frank Baum's work, as well as Tom Mix's screen debut in *Ranch Life in the Great South-West*. Approximately a year after its 1909 inception, Turner joined Carl Laemmle's IMP Company, and when the producer formed Universal Pictures in 1912, Otis Turner became perhaps the most prominent, and certainly the most trusted, director with the new organization. Like Frank Lloyd, he was equally at ease as a screenwriter, and like his protégé, he believed strongly that a director needed a keen dramatic faculty.

Otis Turner remained with Universal through 1916, when, following Frank Lloyd, he went under contract to producer William Fox. He stayed little more than a year with Fox before retiring and devoting his time to a decorating business in Hollywood, where he died on March 28, 1918.

In the summer of 1914, Turner made a trip to New York, ostensibly on vacation and also to renew acquaintance with his theatrical colleagues. While Turner was away, Frank Lloyd was offered the opportunity to direct his company of players — the invitation was not unusual in that the studio, with a heavy release schedule of one- and two-reel fictional shorts, routinely promoted directors from its company of players. It is not clear what is the first film that Lloyd directed, but among the group are the farcical *Royal Rogue*, the psychological drama, *As the Wind Blows*, and *The Vagabond*. The last, released on November 1, 1914, features Herbert Rawlinson in a dual role of the title character and a consumptive stranger whom he rescues from drunken toughs. When the stranger dies, the vagabond adopts his identity and is accepted by the mother who is conveniently blind and on her sick bed. Only following the mother's death and the vagabond's return to the family after leaving to make good does he reveal the truth, which, it transpires, the stranger's sister, now in love with the vagabond, and his father had known all along. *The Vagabond* is melodrama at its best, and it would be nice to believe that it is perhaps Frank Lloyd's first film as a director.

The first prominent film with which Lloyd was associated as director is *The Bachelor's Baby*, in which a child-loving bachelor offers to purchase a baby from its "little mother" for fifty cents. "Lloyd does good work in Turner's absence," reported the studio house journal, *The Universal Weekly* (September 19, 1914), noting that Lloyd had been personally selected by Otis Turner as his temporary replacement.

On November 14, 1914, *The Universal Weekly* made it official, announcing that Frank Lloyd was to be given a post as director of a new company at Universal to be organized especially for him. George Larkin was to be the leading man, Helen Leslie the leading lady, and Marc Robbins, the character man, with the films released under the Rex brand. Lloyd was to continue his work as an actor, taking on the "heavy character leads" in the films he was to direct. The company of players assigned to Lloyd is most certainly not from the upper echelon of Universal actors and actresses. The leading lady has no reputation, while George Larkin's biggest claim to fame is as the leading man in a handful of serials from the 1910s. The only positive aspect of Lloyd's promotion to director was his quickly moving from the Rex to the Laemmle brand, with the use of the studio head's name implying a more prominent production.

In the only feature article on Frank Lloyd to appear in *The Universal Weekly*, the director spoke at length on the change in career and on the

Frank Lloyd, with clipboard, at Universal in 1915; to his left is Miss Universal City.

approach to filmmaking that he was to maintain through to the end of his working life:

"When Otis Turner went East on his vacation last summer, and I was put in charge of his company as substitute director, I was perhaps the happiest man with Universal. Not particularly because of the honor of having been chosen from among so many capable players to handle such a company (although that in itself was enough nearly to turn my head), but because I knew that at last I was going to have a chance to test to my own satisfaction, at least, a theory I had long held regarding the successful production of pictures. In my mind I had reached the conclusion, after much study, that regardless of the players, the director, the cameraman and the scenery, the backbone of every successful production, the foundation upon which was built the finished product, was the story. In my mind, I had set up the word 'story' as a sort of motto, for I felt that while all the other things were necessary, the story was the framework, the skeleton upon which were to be built the draperies that result in good pictures."[7]

As a director at Universal, Lloyd first became attracted to the melodrama, its value as entertainment and the opportunity that it offered for character development. The melodrama as spectacle was somewhat beyond the resources of both director and studio at this time, but all other elements were in place: "I wanted to see if there could not be put on the screen a type of quiet, true-to-life story that made its appeal less to the spectator's excitability than to his sympathies and tenderer [sic] emotions — the type of story which may be found in the best magazines — the establishment of a character or a group of characters, good, bad or indifferent, and then having established the type of individual, having him do what he would be most likely to do under given circumstances."[8]

Typical of Lloyd's Universal melodramas is *The Come-Back*, featuring Lloyd as a convict, released from prison and returning to his wife and family. En route, he encounters a former criminal colleague attempting to rape a young woman. The convict rescues the woman, but is arrested by the police. Because of his previous record, a court finds him at fault and he returns to prison. The come-back never reaches home. All the elements of good melodrama are here, the hero accused of a crime he has not committed, a young woman at risk, and a tragic ending. "The ending is not particularly happy," reported *The Universal Weekly* (March 20, 1915), "but it is too often the way of the world and if there are tears in the eyes of the audiences as they see the picture run, they will at least know that it is sometimes portrayed as it might reasonably be expected to happen in real life."

The criminal trying to make good is also the central theme of *From the Shadows*, released on June 9, 1915. A notorious crook, now leading an honest life, tries to hide his past from his daughter. When one of the crook's companions in crime, played by Lloyd, is attracted to the daughter and tries to kill her fiancé, the father takes the fatal bullet. The daughter and her lover remain unaware of the father's double life.

One of Lloyd's last films at Universal, *Dr. Mason's Temptation*, released on August 22, 1915, further embraces classic aspects of the melodrama. A young doctor (played by Millard K. Wilson, who worked on more than twenty-four films with Lloyd) is tempted to steal from one of his patients in order to pay for his wife to visit her old home. He resists the impulse, the needed money arrives from an unexpected source, and all ends happily. "Quite entertaining," reported *The Moving Picture World* (September 4, 1915).

In April 1915, Lloyd had voiced his concern that as a British citizen, he was shirking his responsibility to serve his country in the European war that had begun the previous year. He was certainly young enough to have been drafted. Many thought that it was only a matter of time before he returned home. Instead, in the summer of 1915, Lloyd left Universal not to engage in the European conflict, but to join the newly formed Pallas Pictures, Inc., whose films were released on the Paramount program, and which unlike Universal was committed to the production of feature-length subjects only. Pallas was associated, and shared a studio, with the Oliver Morosco Photoplay Co., and, within a matter of weeks, the director was handling productions for both companies. Lloyd's appointment is evidence of the reputation that he had gained within the film industry as a reliable director — and one with a future.

Such an evaluation is supported by a news item in the July 31, 1915 issue of the trade paper *Motography*:

"Frank Lloyd, youngest of the moving picture directors of the first class, has been engaged by the Oliver Morosco Company as director. He has been dynamiting his way up to the front for the past few years by sheer native ability and ahead-of-the-times ideas. The opportunity the present post affords him is all that he needs to gain him recognition as a top notcher."

The first Pallas production and Lloyd's first away from Universal was *The Gentleman from Indiana*, adapted from the Booth Tarkington novel. Released in November 1915, it was a mammoth production indicative of what future Frank Lloyd subjects might be. A small town was built on the Pallas lot and for a nighttime rainstorm effect, 14,000 gallons of water were hauled in from a well three miles away. A circus, a torchlight procession and a 500-person mob scene were all part of the production. A football game was staged at the University of Southern California, with players provided by the Los Angeles Athletic Club. Critical response was positive, with *The Moving Picture World* (October 30, 1915) describing Lloyd as "the young expert who in this elaborate offering proves himself to be one of the most able directors in this country today." The trade paper also quoted the *New York Evening Mail* as stating that for genuine atmosphere and human feeling, it is no exaggeration to say that *The Gentleman from Indiana* is a second *The Birth of a Nation*. "We take our hats off to the director," concluded the *New York Evening Mail* review.

The star of *The Gentleman from Indiana*, along with the later Lloyd-directed Pallas production *David Garrick*, is Dustin Farnum, a prominent stage actor who had come to fame in 1903 in the original theatrical production of *The Virginian*, and who later starred on screen in 1914 in both the latter and the first film presentation of *The Squaw Man*. Lloyd was soon to direct Dustin's brother William Farnum in the first of his great screen melodramas, *A Tale of Two Cities*.

In the meantime, Lloyd and Dustin Farnum were proving a successful team. The screen adaptation of the 1864 play on the life of the eighteenth century London actor, David Garrick, must have been most appealing

Dustin Farnum, Frank Lloyd's first star.

to Lloyd. He was able to replicate the Theatre Royal, Drury Lane, and tried, with perhaps only limited success, to capture the drama and spirit of London in the mid 1700s, including a number of exterior scenes. Unfortunately, however, both the play and Dustin Farnum's acting proved dated, and upon the film's New York opening at the Strand Theatre on April 30, 1916, the *New York Times* (May 1, 1916) complained that the actor belonged to "the heaving bosom school of film….Mr. Farnum apparently learned the business when a reasonably good looking man with a nerve to make faces at the camera was made a hero. So as David Garrick he knits his brows, shows his teeth when he smiles and struts with the assurance of a matinee idol of the early 90s." Writing in *Photoplay* (July 1916), Julian Johnson described the play as "ancient" and an "unusual vehicle" for its star.

The trade papers were far more sympathetic. *Motion Picture News* (May 6, 1916) noted that David Garrick proved that "the costume drama is by no means dead." *The New York Dramatic Mirror* (April 26, 1916) described the film as "a delightful comedy drama," and had "high commendation" for Lloyd's direction. The *Mirror* went on to note that the director "seems to have instilled into his players the manners, customs and spirits of those times." It may well be that Lloyd instilled a little too much of theatrical melodrama into the production, ignoring the demands of twentieth century audiences and critics.

Dustin Farnum was not the only stage performer with whom Frank Lloyd worked at the beginning of his career as a feature-length director. Among the eleven films made for either Pallas or Oliver Morosco are *Jane*, released in December 1915 and starring singer-dancer Charlotte Greenwood in her screen debut; *Tongues of Men*, released in January 1916, and *The Code of Marcia Gray*, released in March 1916, and both starring the formidable British actress Constance Collier; the French farce, *Madame La Presidente*, released in February 1916 and featuring the first Mrs. Florenz Ziegfeld, Anna Held, in a stunningly engaging performance; and *The Intrigue*, released in October 1916, and starring Lenore Ulrich, whom David Belasco had fashioned into a major Broadway star.

For his penultimate production for the Pallas/Morosco companies, *The Stronger Love*, released in August 1916, Lloyd returned to acting, playing opposite leading lady Vivian Martin in her first film under a contract with Morosco. The role was typical of the rugged parts that Lloyd had played at Universal, a member of a family of moonshiners, whose brother is engaged to the Vivian Martin character.

Frank Lloyd might be in the early stages of his career as a film director, but he was proving himself not only a good judge of story material, but also someone with whom a stage actor or actress might feel comfortable. He was always sympathetic to the legitimate theatre and to what it represented, while understanding the need of the motion picture for spectacle and for strong production values. It is immediately apparent that all of Frank Lloyd's first major feature films starred actors and actresses from the legitimate stage. They were the performers with whom Lloyd felt comfortable, and who were best suited to his type of productions. In fact, in a 1923, Lloyd had noted that "First and most important is stage experience. While there are a few exceptions, the majority of our best players have been recruited from the stage."[9]

Working with the actors was an integral part of Lloyd's work as a director. The most important part of his job was "to try and inspire the players. When I go to work on a picture, I work on the script too. I want to know those characters so well that I know where the hero would hang his hat, what his bed would look like, how he'd eat. Then I want to see that the player has the same knowledge of his character."[10]

Frank Lloyd was always concerned with the entire production, from the writing of the script through to the final cut. As he explained in the 1930s,

"The public thinks a director is a person who sits and tells actors what to do. That's what the public thinks a director is and it's far from the truth. A director is a man who, if he is worth his salt, takes hold of the job when it's a baby, nurses it along, gets it into a script he can shoot, picks out his sets, selects his people and the small part of the task is telling them what to do.

"What he mainly requires is common sense, good taste along with plenty of hard work and not even a dab of genius. Likewise, he must realize that every six months the whole movie business rolls over and is no longer what it used to be."[11]

Everything that Frank Lloyd did in the mid 1910s was to have relevance to his later career. *The Gentleman from Indiana* tested the mettle of the director who was to make *Wells Fargo* and *The Howards of Virginia*. *David Garrick* may well be considered a precursor to *Cavalcade*, while the temperamental stage actresses whom he directed then served as training for such similarly inclined screen performers as Corinne Griffith whom he was to handle a decade later.

1. Some sources indicate that Lloyd began his career with Mack Sennett's Keystone Company, but this would not appear to be correct. At least two sources claim that it was Charlie Chaplin, who began his career with Mack Sennett, who suggested that Lloyd try his luck as an actor in the United States; in that Lloyd himself made no reference to this, the story is believed to be apocryphal.

2. With the Tide, p. 44.

3. Ibid.

4. The direction of this production is sometimes credited to Frank Lloyd, but, according to The Universal Weekly, it was directed by William Worthington.

5. Frank Condon, "Mutiny on the Set," p. 66.

6. John R. Woolfenden, "Frank Lloyd Says Time Ripe for 'Great American Film,'" p. C1.

7. "Good Stories Absolutely Necessary to Successful Photo Plays, Says Frank Lloyd," p. 15.

8. Ibid.

9. Elizabeth Lonergan, "Directors I Have Met," p. 39.

10. John R. Woolfenden, "Frank Lloyd Says Time Ripe for 'Great American Film,'" p. C1.

11. Quoted in Frank Condon, "Mutiny on the Set," p. 67.

CHAPTER TWO

Adapting Charles Dickens

Between 1916, and the end of his Pallas career, and 1922, and the start of his contract with First National, Frank Lloyd worked for two major studios, Fox and Goldwyn. He directed a total of twenty-eight feature films, including his first Charles Dickens adaptation, *A Tale of Two Cities*, a major adaptation of Victor Hugo's *Les Miserables*, the Geraldine Farrar vehicle, *The World and Its Woman*, and *Madame X* with Pauline Frederick. It was a crucial period in the director's career, establishing him as one of Hollywood's prominent filmmakers and confirming the type of productions to which he was best suited.

Signing a contract with William Fox late in 1916, Lloyd was appointed head of one of the four companies working at the mogul's Western Avenue Studios in Hollywood. The other companies were headed by Edward Le Saint, Bertram Bracken and Chester and Sidney Franklin. Lloyd's first film for the studio was *Sins of Her Parents*, released in November 1916, and starring Fox contract star Gladys Brockwell. It was in many ways a typical, and relatively cheap screen melodrama of the period, with the actress playing a dual role, that of a mother who goes to work as a dance hall girl in Alaska and the daughter who sets out to find her.

Frank Lloyd's second Fox film, *The Price of Silence*, was important as his first with leading man William Farnum, the younger brother of Dustin.[1] William Farnum was born in Boston on July 4, 1876, and at the age of twelve began his stage career, which culminated, at the start of the twentieth century, in a five-year U.S. tour as *Ben-Hur*. He made his screen debut in 1914 in the Selig production of *The Spoilers*, the first screen adaptation of the Rex Beach novel, famous for its climactic fight between Farnum and Tom Santschi. Farnum had joined the William Fox organization in

1915 and remained with the studio through the spring of 1921, becoming the first actor to earn $10,000.00 a week. In 1925, Farnum was seriously injured during the filming of *A Man Who Fights Alone*, and while he continued acting through into the 1950s, he never again played a leading role. After a career that included more than 120 film appearances, William Farnum died in Los Angeles on June 5, 1953.

William Farnum and Frank Lloyd got on well together. Farnum was a rugged actor but one who took direction easily and never showed temperament. He was, in the words of one writer, "a big, generous, fun-loving boy."[2] The two men adopted a carefree attitude on the set; they were always relaxed and respectful of the other. The first film that the two made together was one very close to its director's heart, the second American screen adaptation of Charles Dickens' *A Tale of Two Cities*. The Vitagraph Company of America had produced an "all-star" three-reel version in 1911, featuring just about everyone in its stock company. In 1935, MGM was to produce what is the best-known version of the novel, starring Ronald Colman.

Lloyd was a devoted Dickensian. A British fan magazine writer reported in 1923,

"One of the joys of his first trip to London, he told me, was the hunting up of the many spots made immortal by the great novelist, and trying to picture how the incidents connected with them happened in real life. And so he was visualizing Dickens pictures long before motion pictures were thought of."[3]

It is also possible that in his youth, Frank Lloyd appeared in a small role with Sir John Martin Harvey in *The Only Way*, the actor's stage adaptation of *A Tale of Two Cities*.

The manner in which Lloyd approached the adaptation was a template for how he would work on similar classic versions in the future:

"I decided it would be more discreet to bring the work of Charles Dickens before — possibly — many million people than the work of Lloyd. For that reason I followed as closely as possible the story of the book. Every historical detail was absolutely correct, all the settings were the result of careful, patient research and the characterizations and theme of the story were transferred to the screen in such a manner as to accurately follow the author's ideas."[4]

William Farnum further endorsed Lloyd's approach:

"I know of no other man who could have accomplished the same results with the story as Frank did. He placed himself absolutely in the background. He grasped the various points of the story with a marvelous appreciation of their dramatic and educational value. Time and time again he withstood the temptation to be spectacular in order to be correct and keep within the spirit of the story."

Lloyd embraced the incidents and characters from Dickens that would best make the transition to the screen. He understood the impossibility of a total adaptation of a novel of such length, initially serialized from April 30 through November 26, 1859, but he was fully aware of the major theat-

William Farnum in A Tale of Two Cities.

rical drama unfolding here, the storming of the Bastille, the freeing of Dr. Manette, and the English and French trials of Charles Darnay. He presents the story in linear form from Paris before the Revolution to Sidney Carton's death on the guillotine. The only major departure from Dickens occurs at the film's conclusion with Charles Darnay and Lucie Manette shown as a happily married couple, with a son named Sidney Carton.

Through double exposure, carefully worked out by cinematographer Billy Foster, who was Lloyd's cameraman throughout his time at Fox, William Farnum is able to play both Charles Darnay and Sidney Carton. Jewel Carmen, one of the best and prettiest of Fox actresses of the period, is ideally suited to the part of Lucie Manette. In all honesty, William Farnum is somewhat too old and certainly too heavy for a romantic lead. As *The New York Dramatic Mirror* (March 24, 1917) noted in its review,

""He is a bit heavy and mature for either of these youthful heroes [Darnay and Carton] but his excellent acting relieves this defect in his appearance." The Vitagraph production brought to public attention and eventual stardom Norma Talmadge, playing a girl in the tumbril with Sidney Carton en route to the guillotine. In the Frank Lloyd version, Florence Vidor plays the same character, and, likewise, went on to stardom.

On its release in March 1917, *A Tale of Two Cities* was widely praised by the critics. *Variety* (March 16, 1917) noted that the novel "has been put on the screen in a manner which holds its spectators spellbound, and stamps it a triumph of the art of making moving pictures." Peter Milne, writing in *Motion Picture News* (March 31, 1917) singled out the director for particular praise:

"Mr. Lloyd in the handling of the scenario and in the production of it has truly earned himself a place in the hall of fame of directors. Better than his masterly handling of the mob scenes, his delightful reproduction of the atmosphere of the period; better than his remarkable double exposure scenes and the selection of proper types, is the manner in which he has handled the plot itself. In so doing he has shown himself a master of picture craft. He has cut at just the right moment, has introduced the sub-plots at a time when their introduction is propitious, and has as a consequence derived from the story every possible atom of suspense. In fact, Mr. Lloyd has almost outdone Dickens. 'Better than the book' is, after all, a silly cry for a book and a picture are not comparable; but here we can say that Mr. Lloyd has translated the original work and endowed his translation with all the color and sentiment of the forerunner."

It is a review of which Frank Lloyd must have been proud, a comment that proved his capability to adapt great works of literature, great works of melodrama for the screen. The writer notes Lloyd's handling of mob scenes, for which the director was quickly to gain a reputation, but as a later writer pointed out, Lloyd "has been especially successful in producing mob scenes of intense realism, and depicting against such backgrounds the most delicate of love stories with strong effects."[5]

After four minor productions together, Lloyd and Farnum, along with leading lady Jewel Carmen, returned to classic literary adaptation with *Les Miserables* from the novel by Victor Hugo. It was the first American version of the novel, produced four years after a highly-praised French adaptation. Unlike *A Tale of Two Cities*, which was shot at the Fox West Coast studios, *Les Miserables* was filmed at Fort Lee, New Jersey, where Lloyd directed at least one other Farnum film, *For Freedom*. (The general idea at Fox seems to have been that J. Gordon Edwards was the corporation's director on the east coast, but when he was working in Los Angeles, he was replaced in

New Jersey by Frank Lloyd.⁶) Again, the storyline was much too long for a motion picture and needed careful adaptation. As Jean Valjean, William Farnum is imprisoned for stealing a loaf of bread to feed to his sister and her children. After nineteen years in jail, he is released and befriended by the Bishop, who testifies on his behalf after he has been robbed by Valjean. Five years later, Valjean has changed his name and is mayor of a small town,

William Farnum, far left, in Les Miserables.

where he is suspected by Javert, an inspector of police, of being the former convict. Valjean returns to prison, escapes and rescues Cosette, the illegitimate daughter of a factory worker. With the French Revolution, Valjean saves Cosette's fiancé, is redeemed by Javert, and dies once Cosette and her fiancé are married. Frank Lloyd makes a cameo appearance in the film as the gendarme who first arrests Jean Valjean.

As always, Lloyd stressed research and careful adaptation:

"I read Victor Hugo's novel six times...and I consulted every print and painting that I could find. The research work alone took several weeks and indeed was not completed until the picture was finished. For instance, even the paper cartridges in use at the time of the French revolution — the kind that are bitten off by the man who is loading his gun — were used in the battle scenes. Of course, they had to be specially made. The priest's candlesticks too, those which Jean Valjean stole, were duplicates of the kind used in France at the date of the story. We found them in an old curio store. We also used the real old French coins of the period. These are mere instances of the detail involved."[7]

For the convict scenes, a reported hundred prisoners were "borrowed" from the New York State Penitentiary. A brigade of U.S. soldiers, stationed in New York, was also utilized.

One of the major problems with the film is that William Farnum fails to age particularly well. As *Variety* (December 7, 1917) pointed out at the time, after nineteen years of imprisonment, he is "still fat and sleek." The trade paper also complained of a weak supporting cast: "A pity so much time, money, and intelligent direction should have been coupled with such mediocre histrionic talent." In all, it was reported that the director shot 75,000 feet of film. The complex storyline resulted in an original production that was much too long for most exhibitors. Initially, the planned release print ran 13,000 feet, somewhat longer than *The Birth of a Nation*, and, based on appropriate projection speed, would probably have required at least two-and-a-half hours of viewing time. William Fox ordered the production cut to 9,781 feet, and then, at the request of exhibitors, to 8,400 feet. Frank Lloyd was not pleased. For the five-week run at New York's Lyric Theatre in January and February 1918, it was the 9,781 foot version than was projected, with audiences paying top prices of one dollar a ticket.

Critical response was generally positive, with, again, Peter Milne in *Motion Picture News* (December 22, 1917) singling out Frank Lloyd for special mention:

"But when all is said and done it is to the director, to Frank Lloyd, that the greatest share of credit should go. His is really a master work, the equal of which there is none. There is not a man with a bigger name in the field than Mr. Lloyd's, who could have bettered his work in any department, and there are few with bigger names — perhaps none now. The excellence of the continuity, the clarity of every piece of action, the realism of the atmosphere of the seventeenth century, and above all, the fact that this picture is still Victor Hugo's belittle all expressions of praise."

When *Les Miserables* opened at New York's Lyric Theatre, the following day, the *New York Times* (December 5, 1917) praised it as "Intelligently directed…quite the best picture that has been seen hereabout for a considerable time."

It was not only melodrama at which the team of Lloyd and Farnum excelled. In 1918, they filmed two Westerns together, both based on Zane Grey novels, adapted by Lloyd, which garnered immense favor with the public. *Riders of the Purple Sage* was released in September 1918, followed by a sequel, *The Rainbow Trail*, released a month later. Both films were remade by Fox in 1925 with Tom Mix considerably more athletic in the William Farnum role.

The one individual not entirely happy with the Lloyd-Farnum pairing was William Fox's production head in Los Angeles, Sol Wurtzel, who

William Farnum, second from left, in Riders of the Purple Sage.

complained that the former has become "arrogant, vain and impossible to talk to" since becoming Farnum's director. "Many times Lloyd has told me he would quit unless pictures he directed were released exactly as they were shipped from Los Angeles." The making of the Zane Grey Westerns was troubling to the studio head in that he had agreed to permit the pair to shoot on location in Arizona, but only if production costs were kept below $100,000.00. To Fox's outrage, when scenes shot at the Grand Canyon for *Riders of the Purple Sage* were "fogged" on developing, Lloyd insisted on returning to shoot retakes at a cost of $6,000.00.[8]

At this same time, Lloyd was perhaps dealing with a personal, emotional issue. He had been receiving a number of notices to enlist from the British Commission. These notices could be ignored in that the director had presented himself to the local U.S. draft board in Los Angeles on August 14, 1917. On November 7, 1917, as "a married man with wife and child," he was "discharged from immediate liability to serve under the present call for military service of the United States."[9]

On June 17, 1918, William Fox wrote to Sol Wurtzel, "I would be very sorry to see a disagreement between Lloyd and the Fox Film Corporation, for I have a high personal regard for him. I would consider that he is acting dirty and mean if he did anything to disturb the condition of the Fox Film Corporation."[10] Lloyd did nothing "dirty and mean" initially, but less than a year later, on March 4, 1919, he announced that he

Ann Forrest and William Farnum in The Rainbow Trail.

had severed his connection with the Fox Film Corporation and that he was to become an independent producer.

The notion of independent production did not become reality, but two months later, it was announced that Lloyd had signed a contract with the [Samuel] Goldwyn Pictures Corporation. One trade paper quite rightly described him as "one of the oldest and at the same time one of the youngest directors in motion pictures."[11] Although it was not released until May 1920, the first of Lloyd's films for Goldwyn was probably *The Silver Horde*, based on the Rex Beach novel, *The Silver Horse*, and featuring Myrtle Stedman as Cherry Malotte, the leading female character in *The Spoilers*. In retrospect, the production seems relatively unimportant, despite location shooting in Washington state.

The first Frank Lloyd film to be released by Goldwyn, in September 1919, was one of his most prominent of the period: *The World and*

Its Woman, starring the operatic Geraldine Farrar and her husband Lou Tellegen. Farrar had been on screen since 1915, generally working under Cecil B. DeMille's direction and was the only opera singer of her generation to make a successful transition to films. *The World and Its Woman* was her first film in California under the Samuel Goldwyn contract. In her 1938 autobiography, Farrar, who was somewhat less polite in old age, praised Lloyd as "a distinguished gentleman who is still making fine and beautiful films today."[12]

Of the film itself, the actress commented, "I never did understand what the title had to do with the tale, but it was not without vigor and interest."[13] Set against a background of the Bolshevik Revolution, *The World and Its Woman* has Farrar cast as an American-born opera singer, seen in the film in a scene from Massenet's *Thais*. With a plot involving an attempt by the Bolsheviks to "nationalize" the leading lady, *The World and Its Woman* is typical of the films in the "Red Scare" cycle that appeared around this time. While heaping only lukewarm praise on the leading lady and leading man, Charles Wood in *Exhibitor's Trade Review* (September 13, 1919) had good things to say about the production as well as praising the story for its warning to the American people: "The play, everything considered, is beyond the usual with its magnificent production and big scenes, and is a good interpretation of what may be expected when Bolshevism gains the upper hand over conservative government."

Aside from *The World and Its Woman*, the most important of Lloyd's Goldwyn films are the four starring Pauline Frederick, and, in particular, *Madame X*, released in September 1920. Frederick's biographer noted that the film "wrote her name indelibly on the scroll of fame. It was Frank Lloyd's direction of this melodrama which helped her to make it the finest performance of her career."[14] The first English-language version of the play had opened in New York in 1910, with Dorothy Donnelly in the title role. However, *Madame X* became inextricably linked to Pauline Frederick, and she repeated her screen success in a 1926 American tour and a 1927 London stage appearance.

"The production builds carefully to its climax," commented *Motion Picture News* (October 9, 1920), noting that it could "justly be hailed as one of the notable film events of the season." The film opened in New York at the Capitol Theatre, and the review the following day in the *New York Times* (September 27, 1920) announced it as "well composed and competently directed." The newspaper's critic went on to note that the wordiness of the original hampered its adaptation to the screen. It was "not so much a play in moving pictures as a printed play with animated illustrations."[15]

Madame X marked the penultimate time that Frank Lloyd worked also as a film's screenwriter. It was the only one of his Goldwyn productions for which he received such credit, a shared one with J.E. Nash. In the future, there was to be a marked departure from the director's insistence on handling a film's adaptation from the printed page or the legitimate stage. Certainly, Lloyd would often work closely with the screenwriter in

Leatrice Joy and Wallace Beery (background) in A Tale of Two Worlds.

the early stages of pre-production, but, whatever his contribution, he no longer took a writing credit. He was, however, a director who believed that a script should indicate far more than dialogue or basic acting requirements. As he explained in 1918,

"Most scripts…devote themselves wholly to the main plot of the story, so that it devolves entirely upon the director to introduce 'business' into a production. Unless a director is extremely careful and watchful he is likely to make his production without putting this incidental stuff into the film. This is especially true if the director adheres religiously to the script. I have found that by planning my 'business' before beginning the film I can arrange it so that it works into the story much better than if I made up my business as the occasion arose."[16]

At the end of 1920, Goldwyn announced that Frank Lloyd would be featured as producer of his own films, and this credit appears on another of the extant Lloyd/Goldwyn features, *A Tale of Two Worlds*, released in March 1921. It is "Directed by Frank Lloyd" with the additional credit "A Frank Lloyd Production," thus giving Lloyd as much name recognition as Samuel Goldwyn. The original story was provided by best-selling novelist Gouverneur Morris, one of the "Eminent Authors" under contract to Goldwyn at this time.

A Tale of Two Worlds is not a major Lloyd production, but it is of interest because of a storyline that begins in the China of 1899, "seething with hatred against all foreigners," and then moves on to San Francisco's modern Chinatown. Here, a tour guide escorts groups of women around the community, reporting on murders and pointing out fake "dope fiends." A plump lady and her husband are persuaded to purchase a newly-made, 1,000-year-old bowl. Also in Chinatown is Sui Sen, the daughter of a benign Western couple, murdered in 1899, and brought to America by their faithful servant, Ah Wing, and passed off as his daughter. As played by Leatrice Joy, it is somewhat hard to believe there can be many who believe she is Chinese if for no other reason that her coy and phony melodramatics are over-emphasized against the subtle underplaying of the few real Chinese in the film and even the Western performers in Chinese guise.

As the tension mounts, in true melodramatic fashion, with Sui Sen about to be married to the evil Ling Jo (played by Wallace Beery), the heroine contemplates suicide but is rescued by Ah Wing's faithful servant and the American hero, Newcombe.

Racial stereotyping abounds, and *A Tale of Two Worlds* is melodrama at its wildest — and best. As the *New York Times* (March 14, 1921) commented, when the film opened at the Capitol Theatre, "Mr. Lloyd is a capable cinematician and the actors, while not particularly Chinese in appearance, are melodramatically expressive." Here is "A thriller which sometimes thrills."

The only other Goldwyn production worthy of a special attention is *The Sin Flood*, released in November 1922, and based on a Scandinavian play by Henning Berger. It is a psychological drama involving an eclectic group of individuals trapped in a Louisiana saloon on the Mississippi River by threatened flood waters. Richard Dix and Helene Chadwick head up the cast as a cotton trader and his estranged chorus girl fiancée. Others represented in the group include the saloonkeeper, two other, older cotton traders, the bartender, a broken-down actor, a defrocked minister, and a waterfront bum. With their deaths imminent, the group reforms only to revert to type once they are saved. In some respects, the film is a precursor to Maxwell Anderson's 1939 play *Key Largo* and the 1948 Warner Bros. production of the same title.

When the film opened at the city's Capitol Theatre, the *New York Times* thought it not as strong as the original source, which, curiously, having been adapted as *The Deluge* for the American stage by Arthur Hopkins, opened simultaneously with the screen version at the Plymouth Theatre on January 27, 1922. *Variety* (November 3, 1922) pointed out that "Instead of a problem play it becomes a romance shining in a world of gloom. The difference is good business. Its fidelity to life is less but its appeal to the sentimental picture fans (which means selling it to its new public) is undoubted." *The Sin Flood* was remade by Lloyd as a 1930 talkie, starring Douglas Fairbanks, Jr., Dorothy Revier and Robert Edeson. It is the only film he chose to remake.

This period in Frank Lloyd's career ends, as it began, with a Charles Dickens adaptation, and with Lloyd as both screenwriter and director, it is very much a prime example of his work not just as a filmmaker but as an auteur. While *The Sin Flood* was opening in New York, simultaneously, at the Strand Theatre, *Oliver Twist*, one of the director's most important films to date, made its debut.

Oliver Twist was a favorite with American producers, having been filmed as a short subject by the Vitagraph Company of America as early as 1909. Nat C. Goodwin was famed in vaudeville for his portrayal of Fagin, which he brought to the screen in a 1912 feature-length production. In 1916, actress Marie Doro played Oliver Twist in a Famous Players-Lasky production, with Tully Marshall as Fagin.

In the title role of the Frank Lloyd production is Jackie Coogan, a child actor who had become an immediate star thanks to his performance opposite Charlie Chaplin in his third film, *The Kid*, in 1921. Coogan's career was directed by his father, along with independent producer Sol Lesser. Following *The Kid*, Coogan had starred in *Peck's Bad Boy*, directed by the mediocre but prolific Sam Wood. In 1922, he made three films, the first two of which, *My Boy* and *Trouble*, were relatively unimportant and both written and directed by Albert Austin. It was the third film that year, *Oliver Twist*, which was to become Coogan's most important starring vehicle after *The Kid*, and the one for which his father sensibly selected Frank Lloyd as both director and screenwriter.

The cast was handpicked by Lloyd, in theory with Coogan, Sr.'s participation, and headed by the brilliant Gladys Brockwell as a perfect Nancy Sikes and Lon Chaney as Fagin. Brockwell's face illustrates the grime and the misery that are her character's life, while Chaney's makeup suggests he is more stupid than villainous and is far removed from the stereotypical, anti-Semitic quality of Alec Guinness's makeup in the 1948 David Lean version. Chaney and Lloyd went back a long way together; at Universal, their dressing rooms were side by side, and Lloyd recalled the actor as "the gentlest of men."[17]

According to Sol Lesser, "For *Oliver Twist* the man I thought most capable of doing it was Frank Lloyd. He and I agreed to independently go through the book to see which of the many incidents should be retained for the picture. By lucky coincidence we selected identical materials."[18]

Jackie Coogan in title role of Oliver Twist.

Lloyd has retained the majority of the familiar Dickens characters although there are eliminations, and worked hard to suggest period London in his settings. The storyline runs from Oliver in the workhouse under the care of Mr. Bumble through his rehabilitation under the protection of Mr. Brownlow. It was reported that Lloyd deliberately selected only incidents in the Dickens story in which he knew Coogan would perform well. There was no suggestion that Oliver Twist should grow up on screen. Jackie Coogan is not a tragic hero. He is just too cute and irresistible — and too young. In fact, Coogan's innate "cuteness" limits somewhat his ability to perform on screen in a naturalistic style, but Lloyd was the child actor's ardent defender against such criticism and the fact that Coogan's character is not as tragic as that in the novel.

"He is not a child prodigy," explained the director. "He is not precocious in the way the word is usually meant. He is utterly natural, absolutely spontaneous and wholly unconscious and unforced. He is a great artist."[19]

Charles Larkin in *Motion Picture News* (November 4, 1922) was equally supportive: "It is nothing less than marvelous this work of Jackie Coogan...

Oliver is Jackie. Take it either way you will. Here is a remarkably well sustained piece of youthful emotions such as we have been wont to expect in former Coogan offerings. To 'arrive' at Jackie's tender age is indeed an achievement. Well, Jackie has 'arrived,' in every sense of the word."

Oliver Twist received relatively weak reviews. *Variety* (November 10, 1923) described it as "Jackie Coogan in a costume play. That about sums

Lon Chaney as Fagin and Gladys Brockwell as Nancy Sikes in Oliver Twist.

up the production. It is a series of characterizations from the pages of Dickens, but hardly enough of Jackie Coogan to please the picture fans." *Variety* wondered if the film might appeal as much to Dickens enthusiasts as Coogan fans, and similarly the *New York Times* (October 30, 1922) asked if it was a Dickens or a Coogan draw: "Jackie Coogan's Oliver Twist is true, somewhat less pathetic, perhaps, than the original Oliver, but appealing nevertheless, a characterization you cannot resist and have no desire to." The *Times* did, however, complain that "the photoplay often seems hurried and sketchy."

One of the most favorable of reviews, concentrating on Lloyd's work, came from prominent critic Robert Sherwood:

"He managed to retain the flavor of the novel, something which is not easy of accomplishment in the movies. Following the career of young

Oliver through the poorhouse, through Mr. Sowerberry's funeral parlors, through the sordid filth of Fagin's quarters in the depths of London, and finally into the peaceful respectability of Mr. Brownlow's delightful home, Lloyd never lost sight of Dickens's scenes and Dickens's weird characters...

"Frank Lloyd has a fine eye for types, and the cast of *Oliver Twist* was as picturesque an assemblage as Hollywood could provide...

"Aside from his fine direction, Lloyd was responsible for the adaptation of the story. It was a terribly difficult task, in view of the fact that Dickens, in *Oliver Twist* as in all his novels, paid considerably more attention to his characters than he did to his narrative. He created his people and then permitted them to wander pretty much as they listed.

"*Oliver Twist* was a coherent story on the screen, and this was entirely due to Frank Lloyd's deft weaving of the various strands of plot."[20]

When *Oliver Twist* was completed, a publicity stunt had the print escorted by a bodyguard to the station in Los Angeles, where, on September 11, 1922, it was put upon the Santa Fe Limited for New York. Sol Lesser accompanied the print back east. Frank Lloyd complained to *The Morning Telegraph* (September 17, 1922) that he had given up two weeks of his vacation to appear at the station. The director then picked up his golf clubs and returned to the links. It was typical of Frank Lloyd that he participated as required in studio publicity but then returned to a private life.

---

1. A third brother, the youngest, Marshall Farnum was also an actor.

2. Carolyn Lowrey, The First One Hundred Noted Men and Women of the Screen, New York: Moffat, Yard, 1920, p. 56.

3. Elizabeth Lonergan, "Directors I Have Met," p. 39.

4. Quoted in E.V. Durling, "A Director with a Conscience," p. 92.

5. "Own Work Reflects Spirit of Directors," p. 215.

6. "Lloyd West — Edwards East," The Moving Picture World, November 17, 1917, p. 1010.

7. Grace Kingsley, "Hugo Classic Soon," Los Angeles Times, January 13, 1918, Section III, p. 1.

8. William Fox to Sol Wurtzel, May 23, 1918, reprinted in Lillian Wurtzel Semenov and Carla Winter, eds., William Fox, Sol M. Wurtzel and the Early Fox Film Corporation: Letters, 1917-1923, Jefferson, N.C.: McFarland, 2001, p. 44.

9. Certificate of Discharge from Military Service in the archives of Frank Lloyd's family.

10. Ibid, p. 45.

11. "Director Frank Lloyd Signs with Goldwyn," The Moving Picture World, May 3, 1919, p. 654.

12. Geraldine Farrar, Such Sweet Compulsion, New York: The Greystone Press, 1938, p. 183.

13. Ibid, p. 183.

14. Muriel Elwood, Pauline Frederick: On and Off the Stage, p. 99.

15. Madame X is preserved by the International Museum of Photography at George Eastman House.

16. "Lloyd Finishes For Freedom," The Moving Picture World, December 17, 1918, p. 1104.

17. With the Tide, p. 49.

18. Quoted, without source, in Michael Pointer, Charles Dickens on the Screen: The Film, Television and Video Adaptations, Lanham, Maryland: Scarecrow Press, 1996, p. 46.

19. Faith Service, "Frank Lloyd's Jackie Coogan," p. 43.

20. Robert Sherwood, The Best Moving Pictures of 1922-23, Boston: Small, Maynard, 1923, p. 35.

Frank Lloyd advises Norma Talmadge on her make-up.

CHAPTER THREE

The Sea Hawk and *The Divine Lady*

By the 1920s, Frank Lloyd was recognized as one of the industry's leading film directors, handling major productions with originality and skill. As the *New York Times* commented in 1923, "Men like Frank Lloyd, Fred Niblo [who was to go on to direct *Ben-Hur*], Rex Ingram, James Cruze [who had just completed *The Covered Wagon*], Marshall Neilan and a few others are not tarred with the imitative brush."[1]

Leaving Goldwyn in 1922, Lloyd became what might basically be described as a semi-independent filmmaker, directing feature films for First National release. Under contract to Joseph Schenck, he directed the producer's wife, Norma Talmadge, one of the great, under-rated dramatic stars of the silent era, in four films: *The Eternal Flame* (1922), *The Voice from the Minaret*, *Within the Law*, and *Ashes of Vengeance* (all 1923). *The Moving Picture World* reported, "all owe a good part of their success to Mr. Lloyd, whose intelligent direction and assiduous attention to detail combined with Norma Talmadge's own innate ability, raised them to a high plane of entertainment. His knowledge of dramatic values; the power of suggestion, and the subtle points of screen directorship are evident in these productions to any student of pictures."[2]

Joseph Schenck spent between $500,000.00 and $750,000.00 on production of *Ashes of Vengeance*, and just as his budget was testimony to his faith in the director, so did First National indicate its approval of Lloyd by placing him under contract to the distribution organization in the summer of 1923. First National president Robert Lieber pointed out that aside from a handful of prominent stars, exhibitors had to depend upon major directors "for the kind of product needed to keep the motion picture progressing in accord with the public demand."[3]

The contract between Lloyd and Associated First National Pictures, Inc., dated July 2, 1923, was a generous one, and again evidence of the director's standing in the industry. It provided for Lloyd's direction of four films, with the distributor's advancing the actual negatives costs, which were not to exceed $250,000.00. $25,000.00 of that amount was to cover Lloyd's services as producer. The distributor was to pay the producer twenty-five percent of the net profits, with a minimum payment per film of $15,000.00. Further, First National agreed to spend $15,000.00 on publicity for each production.

Somewhat flippantly, opera star Geraldine Farrar dismissed Frank Lloyd with the comment, "I liked him as a director, but he had better luck with ships than with people."[4] The 1919 Farrar vehicle, *The World and Its Woman*, may not have been one of Lloyd's greatest achievements, but the fault could well have been as much with the story and not with the people, but rather the opera star involved. While it is positively ludicrous to dismiss Lloyd as an actors' director, there is certainly truth to the suggestion that he was at his best with ships — or more precisely seafaring dramas.

Frank Lloyd had loved anything to do with the sea since childhood, but it was not until *The Sea Hawk* that he was given the opportunity to transfer that affection, in truly awe-inspiring style, to the screen. As one reporter noted, *The Sea Hawk* finally and completely demonstrated Lloyd's certain knowledge of the sea, of ships and of sailors. Certainly, the director had been involved in some earlier seafaring epics. While at Universal, as an actor he had been featured in two 1913 three-reel dramas of the sea, *Captain Kidd* and *The Buccaneers*. The latter, directed by David Hartford, and for which Lloyd also provided the screenplay, dealt with the careers of the English pirate Edward Teach, known as Blackbeard, and the French pirate Jean Laffite. Here, they are presented as partners in crime, despite having lived in different centuries. Lloyd appears as twenty-four-year-old John Archer, a young man pressed into piracy, rather as the hero of *The Sea Hawk* and the supporting players of *Mutiny on the Bounty* are forced into service on board ship. Also at Universal, Lloyd directed and starred as the skipper in the one-reel *The Bay of Seven Isles*, released on March 28, 1915.

Extensive research, which always fascinated the director, began late in 1923. It was supervised by William J. Reiter, with Don Miller preparing blueprints and drawings of properties and settings, and Joseph Delfino overseeing the manufacture of the latter. This was the first film to deal with Moorish history, and it was claimed that months of research was necessary into the details of life in Morocco and Algeria in the early

1500s. Harry E. Weil, the general manger of Lloyd's company, scoured Pacific Coast seaports for ships' hulls that might be transformed into the Barbary Coast pirates' corsair galleys and the Spanish argosies. Lloyd was determined that his production would contain no shots of miniature ships floating in a tank.

In January 1924, Lloyd built an extensive so-called location camp on the West Side of Catalina Island, eighteen miles from the city of Avalon. It was reported that 150 tents were erected to house the company of 600 principals, extras, technicians, and sailors, with some eighteen men designated to provide meals for the company. Four 16th Century ships were built to scale and transported to Catalina from a dry dock in San Pedro.[5] For the Spanish galleon, a 172-feet long sailing ship was refurbished, with room for a crew of one hundred. An old ferryboat was used as the foundation for the Moorish galleon, with a length of 175 feet.[6]

Also in January 1924, Lloyd selected Milton Sills to play the lead role of Sir Oliver Tresssilian, who will later become Sakr-el-Bahr, "The Sea Hawk." It is splendid casting with the much under-rated Sills displaying the strength of character ideal for the role. As the *Los Angeles Times* (June 8, 1924) commented, *The Sea Hawk* was "likely to do for Milton Sills what *The Four Horsemen* [*of the Apocalypse*] did for Valentino." Sills is no typical leading man, no slight, romantic lead, but rather an actor of stature, whose entire body suggests strength and vitality no matter the characterization. Ironically, the actor's last screen appearance prior to his untimely death in 1930 was in another seafaring picture, *The Sea Wolf*.

After five weeks of filming on sea and at Catalina, the company moved to dry land, and to the United Studios (now the Paramount Pictures lot). Here, an Algerian city and slave market was constructed. It was claimed that $85,000.00 was spent on costuming, and a dozen make-up artists were hired to work under the supervision of Ernest Westmore (of the famous Westmore family).

The Sea Hawk boasts a good supporting cast, led by Lloyd Hughes, also signed in January 1924, in an unusual characterization as Sills' cowardly half brother, Wallace Beery, Frank Currier, and William Collier, Jr. The pressbook describes Wallace Beery's role as that of "The boldest, wickedest, merriest pirate that ever spat in a galley ditch — who roved the seas for booty, kidnapped fair damsels and lolled in Moorish Harems — the roaringest ruffianly rascal that ever scuttled ship or stole a maiden's heart." Presumably, the actor had fun with his character, although it is far more subdued role than the above description might suggest. Less happy in his participation was poor Lloyd Hughes, who almost died during the filming of a scene off San Pedro. While swimming in the ocean, he swallowed oil that had been jettisoned by one of the ships in port, or perhaps from a speedboat that was filming the action, and was forced to recuperate at home for many days.

There can be little disagreement that this is Hughes' best screen role, one with substance and one in which he plays against character. His daughter confirms that her father was particularly happy with the part

Left to right: James Cooley, Lloyd Hughes, Claire Dubrey, and Wallace MacDonald in The Sea Hawk; *Dubrey is particularly well cast in the small role of "The Siren."*

and filled with praise for Frank Lloyd, whom he regarded as a "strong" director.[7]

The *Los Angeles Times* (June 8, 1924) considered Enid Bennett, as the love interest for both Sills and Hughes, "hopelessly miscast" and "too placid," instead preferring Ann Harding or Dorothy Mackaill. In fact, she is adequate, at best but, then, the film really doesn't need an overpowering, strong leading lady. It's a man's film through and through, with just the right amount of romantic masculinity to appeal also to a female audience. It may very well be that the casting of Enid Bennett, who had been Douglas Fairbanks' leading lady in *Robin Hood* (1922), had much to do with the obvious effort to promote Milton Sills as the swashbuckling equal of Fairbanks. Truth be told, Sills is arguably a better actor than

Fairbanks, but the film fails to deliver him as a swashbuckling hero — his character is too complex for that and his stunts are not as ambitious as those of Fairbanks.

Frank Lloyd's name appears twice in the opening credits. Above the title, the film is identified as a presentation of Frank Lloyd Productions, Inc., while the last title card identifies it as personally supervised and directed by Frank Lloyd. *The Sea Hawk* may very well be Frank Lloyd's concept, but the storyline closely follows the novel by Rafael Sabatini. And if anything, it is Sabatini's convoluted plot, presented in considerable detail, which slows the production down and prevents Lloyd from demonstrating much vigor in his direction.

The son of an English mother and an Italian father, Rafael Sabatini (1875-1950) was one of the most popular writers of romantic adventure novels of his day. Indeed, based on his coverage on the internet, he still boasts a widespread following to the present. Several of his novels formed the basis for popular motion pictures, beginning with *Scaramouche* in 1923, followed by *Captain Blood* and *The Sea Hawk*, all of which were filmed as talkies far less faithful to their original sources. *Scaramouche* was directed by Rex Ingram, and is an irritatingly slow-paced film. Frank Lloyd follows very much in Ingram's footsteps, carefully composing each shot with seemingly disregard for action or strong drama. The two men are surprisingly close in style despite very different backgrounds and personalities.

Were Frank Lloyd and Rafael Sabatini close in their outlooks on the world? Both men certainly displayed a sense of adventure in their work. Both were romanticists. There was even an announcement from First National, reported in the trade publication *Filmograph* (April 19, 1930), that Lloyd was to film *Captain Blood* as a sequel to *The Sea Hawk*. One can only wonder if the director was attracted by Sabatini's comment that "There remained the sea, which is free to all, and particularly alluring to those who feel themselves at war with humanity."

The Sea Hawk is a long film — some thirteen reels in length — and its opening four reels are unquestionably slow and heavy in plot. Following a nice opening shot of the sea and waves breaking on the shore, the central English characters, all living in Cornwall in the far west of the country, are introduced: Milton Sills as Sir Oliver Tressilian, in love with Enid Bennett as Rosamund Goldolphin, her guardian Sir John Killigrew (Marc MacDermott) and her brother Peter Godolphin (Wallace MacDonald), both of whom disapprove of the relationship, and Lloyd Hughes as Oliver's half-brother Lionel, who is something of a coward and also in love with Rosamund. There are considerable heroic speeches, such as

Rosamund's prescient declaration to Oliver that "Our love is God's gift. It will endure though men part us and the seas divide."

There is a duel, foolish women who play one man against another, and who demand promises that cannot be kept. Sir Oliver is accused of killing Peter Godolphin, who was actually killed by his half-brother in a duel. Fearing that he will be arrested and punished, and hoping to place blame

Milton Sills and Albert Prisco, foreground, show off their muscles in The Sea Hawk.

for the death on Sir Oliver, Lionel hires Jasper Leigh (Wallace Beery) to kidnap his half-brother and carry him off to sea in his ship, *The Swallow*. Beery's character is described as having "never violated his conscience because he didn't have any," but, in reality, he does allow the promise of extra money from Sir Oliver to permit him to confess to what has happened and to agree to return the nobleman to England. "Thou art most foully abused."

Before his can happen, *The Swallow* is attacked by a Spanish galleon and the crew, including Sir Oliver, taken prisoner. Sir Oliver is ordered "to the oars" and finds himself "a slave to Spain." As Sir Oliver is shown at the oars, stripped down to a loincloth, we are told that "His body, hardened by the grueling toil, became as tempered steel; his soul a cauldron of smoldering hate." As he watches his Spanish conquerors on the bridge, he cries, "If these be Christian, then do I call God to witness I renounce the name."

His declaration impresses Sir Oliver's fellow oarsman, Yusuf-Ben-Moktar. As the two men comfort each other in their pain and suffering, Lloyd cuts to a shot of Lionel and Rosamund kissing.

In what is undoubtedly the best sea battle in the film, involving stren-

Enid Bennett and Milton Sills in The Sea Hawk.

uous hand-to-hand fighting, the Spanish galleon is seized by a Moorish pirate, Asad-ed-Din, the Basha of Algiers (well played by Frank Currier), who turns out to be the uncle of Yusuf-Ben-Moktar. The latter is killed by an arrow fired by a Spanish sniper up in the sails and avenged by Sir Lionel. Asad-ed-Din recognizes the English nobleman as "ripened for Allah's service by Christian's inhumanity to Christian." At the start of reel seven, Sir Lionel has now become Sakr-el-Bahr, "Hawk of the Sea." He tries, without success, to get a message back to England through Jasper Leigh. When this fails, he sets sail for Cornwall, disrupts the marriage of Lionel and Rosamund and takes them back as slaves to what is presumably Algiers.

Lionel and Rosamund are put up for sale at a slave auction. Lionel is stripped and sent to the oars, while Sir Oliver marries Rosumund under Moslem law rather than allow her to become the slave of Asad-ed-Din. There are plot complications delivered by one of the latter's wives and her young son, all of which could easily have been dropped from the film. Rosamund is smuggled aboard Sir Lionel's boat. When Sir John Killigrew's more substantial vessel is spotted, Lionel is persuaded by Sir Oliver to swim to it, and to have Killigrew negotiate with Asad-ed-Din for the English couple to be released to him. A convenient deathbed confession from Lionel resolves the plot, and the film concludes with Killigrew's and Tressilan's estate combined with the marriage (presumably now a Christian one) of Rosamund and Sir Oliver. Jasper Leigh has become a faithful retainer, with the couple's young son on his knee, recounting how his exploits saved the boy's father.

The money that went into the production has been well spent on the sailing vessels, the careful selection of English-looking locations and the Moorish city with its slave market. Costumes are, as far as one can ascertain, realistic to the period, although perhaps seeming a little too effete for the men. Of course, it is the men who dominate, and quite frankly the film really gets going once they take their shirts off. Sills and Hughes both show off their torsos, with Sills easily the winner in terms of muscle and toning. There is even an earlier scene wherein the Sills character asks Justice Anthony Baine to examine his body to show there is no wound and thus he did not duel with Peter Godolphin. Apparently nude except for a ankle-length robe, Sills proudly exposes his upper half to the camera. The actor looks good in a loincloth, but even he does not expose as much of his body as Albert Prisco, playing Yusuf-Ben-Moktar.

Praise for *The Sea Hawk* was lavish and came from all quarters. One trade paper, *Harrison's Reports* (June 14, 1924) announced that it was a film "that elevates the motion picture industry, and the art." Most critics singled out the battle scenes, with *Photoplay* (August 1924) writing, "The hand-to-hand combats between the fighting ships of the day are done with spirit and skill by Director Frank Lloyd. These moments, in fact, seem to be the best he has given the screen since he made *The Tale of Two Cities*. These galley moments are remarkable. The huge battlecraft with their masses of almost naked humanity chained to the oars, sweltering under the hot Mediterranean sun, are graphic in their realism." After the production's New York opening at the Astor Theatre, the *New York Times* (June 2, 1924) announced, "This is far and away the best sea story that has ever been brought to the screen," noting that it "has the distinct advantage of having been directed by Frank Lloyd, an experienced and imaginative producer with a love of realism." At the start of a run of more than two months at the Criterion Theatre in Los Angeles, Edwin Schallert in the *Los Angeles Times* (July 3, 1924) compared it to D.W. Griffith's *Intolerance*, and wrote, "It rivals some of the very finest spectacles that have ever been made."

So popular was the film that Mack Sennett produced a two-reel comedy titled *The Sea Squawk*. It is not a burlesque of the original production, but, perhaps in silent tribute to its director, the short did star Harry Langdon as an immigrant Scotsman.

Following completion of *The Sea Hawk*, Lloyd took a break from major productions, directing five relatively unimportant feature films for First National release. Released four months after *The Sea Hawk*, *The Silent Watcher* is a minor domestic drama starring Glenn Hunter and Bessie Love whose marriage is threatened by the husband's misplaced loyalty to a candidate for U.S. Senate. Marital misunderstandings are also dominant in *Her Husband's Secret*, starring Antonio Moreno and Patsy Ruth Miller, and released in February 1925. Anna Q. Nilsson and Ben Lyon star in a melodrama of the Alaskan Gold Rush, *Winds of Chance*, released in August 1925. The Gold Rush also serves as a background for *The Splendid Road*, again starring Anna Q. Nilsson, released in December 1925. All four films were scripted by J.G. Hawks, who had also worked with Lloyd on *The Sin Flood* and *The Sea Hawk*. Adela Rogers St. Johns adapted the Jules Furthman story *The Wise Guy* for the screen; a melodrama involving medicine men and evangelists, starring Mary Astor and James Kirkwood, it was released in May 1926.

The last four of these films were described as "big productions," and it was announced that Lloyd "has read and analyzed more than one hundred stories, books and plays before making his selection for new picture plays."[8] The end result hardly justifies this claim. Even more astonishing is a report that First National budgeted $1.5 million for Lloyd's 1925 productions, compared to one million dollars for those of George Fitzmaurice and $350,000.00 for those of John Stahl.[9]

From First National, Lloyd moved on to Paramount, which magnanimously pointed out in its publicity that *The Sea Hawk* "was justly acclaimed as the greatest photoplay of its kind that had ever been brought to the screen." And so, it was only natural that Lloyd should return to his beloved ocean and to a period drama with *The Eagle of the Sea*, set in 1815, on land in New Orleans, and on water with a group of French patriots attempting to rescue Napoleon from St. Helena while Jean Lafitte plies his piracy. Florence Vidor is a beautiful Southern Belle and Ricardo Cortez plays the pirate in this adaptation of Charles Tenney Jackson's novel *Captain Sazarac*. It is not a great film, in part because Ricardo Cortez is miscast and also because it is a drama without much drama. And Charles Tenney Jackson is no Rafael Sabatini.

What reviewers found most to praise were the sequences at sea. "Mr. Lloyd has gone to no little trouble in his sea scenes," noted Mordaunt

Hall in the *New York Times* (November 17, 1926), after the film's opening at the Rivoli Theatre. While admitting that "The sea fights are well done," *Variety* (November 17, 1926) had to admit that "The picture is good enough entertainment in its way but does not stand out as something extraordinary, which was expected from Lloyd." In some respects, *The Eagle of the Sea* was comparable to Douglas Fairbanks' *The Black Pirate*, but it lacked audience appeal.

Corinne Griffith is unquestionably one of the most beautiful of silent stars, with a facial delicacy that led to her being described as "The Orchid of the Screen." "The camera loves her" is a phrase that might have been written of Corinne Griffith. She had started her career with the Vitagraph Company in the mid 1910s and quickly became a star, at the height of her screen fame in the 1920s. After a few sound productions, she retired and in later years, she became a wealthy businesswoman with a number of books to her credit. She also became rather eccentric, denying in court that she was the same Corinne Griffith who had starred in silent films.

Frank Lloyd and Corinne Griffith first worked together in 1923 on the screen adaptation of California writer Gertrude Atherton's most famous novel, *Black Oxen*. The title is taken from a poem by W.B. Yeats, "The years, like great black oxen, tread the world, and God, the herdsman, goads them on behind." It is a story of rejuvenation, of a mysterious and beautiful woman, played by Corinne Griffith, who has restored her youth through medical treatment. She is loved by a playwright, played by Conway Tearle, but, ultimately realizes the folly of marrying him and returns to her native Austria, thus allowing her lover to marry a flapper, played by Clara Bow. It is particularly nice casting to have Bow here appearing as everything that the older woman, Corinne Griffith, would like to be, but without the maturity of mind that the latter still retains.

As to Lloyd's casting of her, Clara Bow recalled, "He didn't try t'make me think I didn't have no chance an' that he was doin' me a favor lettin' me work in his picture. When I came inta his office, a big smile came over his face. He told me I was just what he wanted."[10]

Supporting the leading players was a number of Los Angeles society women, all of whom presumably would have welcomed the rejuvenation treatment propagandized by Gertrude Atherton. According to *The Morning Telegraph* (September 20, 1923), the women donated their $7.50 checks to the charitable Los Angeles Assistance League.

The screen rights to the novel were purchased for $25,000.00 in February 1923, and subsequently sold by Warner Bros., the successor company to First National, in September 1931 to MGM for a mere $13,000.00, including all rights to the silent version. MGM never did produce a remake. The film cost a little over $374,000.00 to produce, and, as of August 1924, it had grossed over $570,000.00.[11]

Critical response to *Black Oxen* was mixed, with *Variety* (January 10, 1924) commenting, "While it may have had value as literature, there is nothing outstanding to recommend it for screen entertainment." When the film opened at New York's Strand Theatre, the *New York Times*

Frank Lloyd, unidentified, and Corinne Griffith on the set of The Black Oxen.

(January 7, 1924) hailed it as "a brilliant example of faithful adherence to an intensely interesting narrative."

Frank Lloyd was to make two other films with Clara Bow, *Children of Divorce* and *Hoop-La*, which was the actress' farewell to the screen. The latter, released in November 1933, was a remake of the 1928 film, *The Barker*, which was based on the 1927 play of the same name by John Kenyon Nicholson. Bow is cast in the role of Lou, a cooch dancer in a carnival, a role played earlier, with considerable vigor and cynicism, by Dorothy Mackaill. Her love interest is provided by Richard Cromwell, reprising the role originally played by Douglas Fairbanks, Jr.

Hoop-La is inferior to *The Barker*, and Bow was not particularly happy in her part. In the process of requiring cuts suggestive of a sexual relationship between her and Cromwell's character, a staff member at the Production Code Administration had to confess that "The picture provides a colorful role for Miss Bow"[12] In her November 24, 1933 syndicated column, Louella Parsons, while admitting the film was "not what one might call an intellectual treat," praised Lloyd for "some of the excellent carnival stuff" and Bow for "the sheer force of her personality." When the film opened at New York's Roxy Theatre, B.R. Crisler in the *New York Times* (December 1, 1933) also praised Bow's acting, but criticized the direction and adaptation, pointing out the actress needed more "tactful supervision" than she received here.

Lloyd and Corinne Griffith were reunited in 1928 on *The Divine Lady*, for which the director was paid $30,000.00.[13] Lloyd was well worth the money; he was capable of handling the star, despite an accurate description of her at the time by *Los Angeles Times* writer Harry Carr that "She is a lady who gets her way — never losing her poise or her dignity; but never losing her predominance of the situation either."[14] The film marked Griffith's return to First National after an unhappy period with United Artists. Producer credit for the film went to Griffith's husband Walter Morosco, whom she had married in 1924 and who was the son of theatrical producer Oliver Morosco, although his contribution to the actual production was, in all probability, slight if non-existent.

The Divine Lady had been a 1924 novel by E. Barrington, writing under the nom-de-plume of L. Adams Beck. The screen rights were acquired in December 1927 for a mere $10,000.00, with an additional $1,200.00 paid in August 1928 for the sound rights. From the start, there was concern that the story dealt with the relationship between a married man, Nelson, and his mistress, Emma Hamilton. The studio concept was that Emma's love affair was motivated by patriotism and love of country. As First National production manager Richard A. Rowland in New York explained it, in almost illiterate fashion, to W.R. Rothacker at the studio in January 1928,

"here is a strong love story between a man and a woman, the woman being his mistress and this incidentally being very delicately treated…

"We must be very careful to see that we do not offend the English because Nelson is a great figure in England and this woman being his mistress, unless treated with a patriotic background for her affection, is apt to offend…

"I want to impress upon [Al] Rockett and Morosco the necessity of getting sex and love angle in this picture realizing Lloyd's lack of love interest and sex appreciation so it is up to these two birds to see that Lloyd gets this in. For the virility of the picture I do not think we could get a more ideal man than Frank, likewise for working within a budget."[15]

Lloyd certainly provided the necessary "virility," but such provision led in large part to the film's going over budget. *The Divine Lady* was an expensive production, not only in terms of studio sets but also, and more prominently, the effort to avoid use of miniatures for the battle scenes and to employ two warships, the Victory and the Vanguard.

Both were built at Craig's Shipyard in Long Beach for $245,000.00 — both were budgeted at $155,000.00. As was explained, "At the time the budget was made the plan of the director was to have a complete Victory and just the profile of the Vanguard as atmosphere during the battle. As the picture developed both vessels had to be completely rigged, and as a matter of fact the Vanguard was used every day during the shooting and for more scenes than the Victory."[16] A company of ninety arrived at "The Isthmus" on Santa Catalina Island on June 1, 1928. The Isthmus Company was paid $500.00 a day for the use of the location, on which were erected 100 tents, each with two beds, but only five shower baths. In actual cost, it was estimated that the shooting on Santa Catalina Island cost between $10,000.00 and $12,000.00 a day. There are some shots of miniatures used for the battle scenes, which look surprisingly good, and these were filmed at a special reservoir built on the studio lot in Burbank by the Fitzgerald Engineering & Construction Co. for $6,800.00 between May 4 and May 23, 1928.

According to the film's pressbook, it was eight months in production, with Corinne Grifith's appearing in forty-eight different costumes and Victor Varconi, as Lord Nelson, in eighteen. Two full-time make-up men were employed throughout the production, along with two hairdressers and fifteen additional make-up people for the battle sequences. *The Divine Lady* was the fourteenth sea picture on which Frank Lloyd had worked, and the same number of assistant directors was employed for the battle scenes.

Victor Varconi's salary varied between $800.00 and $1,250.00 a week, payable to the Cecil B. DeMille Pictures Corporation, to which he was under contract. Marie Dressler, as Mrs. Hart, received $2,000.00 a week; Ian Keith, as the Honorable Charles Greville, received $1,250.00 a week; Montagu Love, as Captain Hardy, received $1,000.00 a week; Michael Vavitch, as King Ferdinand, received $500.00 a week; Dorothy Cumming, as Queen Maria Carolina, received $600.00 a week; Evelyn Hall, as the Duchess of Devonshire, received $350.00 a week.

Frank Lloyd for once did not keep within either budget or shooting schedule. Fifty days were spent filming at the studio — four more than had been anticipated. The battle scenes took three instead of two weeks. Strong winds forced all crew members from aloft the sailing ships and a break in filming. Corinne Griffith was taken ill during production, which resulted in lost time. There were eleven weeks from the start of shooting until the end of location work in Long Beach, and there were still the miniature battle scenes and the retakes to be shot at the studio. The initial draft budget for the film was $1,195,829.00. Prior to filming, this was reduced to $885,000.00, but, ultimately, *The Divine Lady* cost $1,110,000.00.

For the role of Sir William Hamilton, Norman Trevor was to receive $1,000.00 a week. However, the night before shooting was to commence, Trevor was arrested and placed in the Psychopathic Ward of the Los Angeles County Hospital and adjudged insane.[17] An affidavit of insanity had been filed against Trevor by his friend H.B. Warner, and it was H.B. Warner who took over the role of Sir William Hamilton for a much higher salary — $2,000.00 a week. One can only surmise that Warner took over the role out of friendship for Trevor, and not because he coveted the part and so had his friend committed. Norman Trevor's career was ended, and he died of a "brain malady" at the Norwalk, California, State Insane Hospital, on October 31, 1929.[18]

Some 150 or 200 extras appeared in the battle scenes, and, in their number, is Robert Parish, who was to become an Academy Award-winning editor (*Body and Soul*) and director. Twelve years of age, he had promoted himself as Nelson's drummer boy, despite having no sense of rhythm, and also suffering from seasickness. As he recalled,

"Thornton Freeland, the first assistant director, was rehearsing the scene with Miss Griffith and two hundred extras, including two lifeguards from State Beach in Santa Monica (Joel McCrea and Andy Devine) and a nervous drummer boy (me). As Lady Hamilton was received by Captain Hardy (Montagu Love), Jimmy Townsend [assistant to the director] yelled, 'Start the drum role!' and I did the best I could, which wasn't good enough. In fact, it was terrible...It took Frank Lloyd about fifteen seconds to discover that a serious casting mistake had been made."

Parish was demoted to "powder monkey" at half pay. "I tried to stay as close to Frank Lloyd as possible," he wrote, "because everything seemed to stem from him. I remember him as a man of complete authority, with bushy eyebrows hovering over deep blue, penetrating eyes...he actually used his megaphone." He and the other boys on the film were schooled on location by a gentleman named Francis Slayton, who tried to instill in them a knowledge of Lord Nelson and his career: "When he told us about Nelson's death and 'Kiss Me Hardy,' which we had seen acted out (with Montagu *Love* playing Hardy), we concluded that we were in with a bunch of fairies. We invented endless jokes about queers. The fact that our schoolroom was stuck away in a corner of the 'poop' deck didn't escape our attention either...I never had a better summer in my whole life. I think of Mr. Slayton every time I pass Trafalgar Square, and I have never said no to a casting director."[19]

Beautiful as is Corinne Griffith and as fine her performance, it is the actress who proved the biggest problem to the film, not because of her temperament (and she was certainly temperamental) but because of her voice. The film was released as a Vitaphone sound-on-film presentation with music and sound effects. It was also to have contained seven talking sequences. There was an obvious problem in that Lord Nelson was played by a Hungarian, whose British accent would have been a joke. Also, as filming of these talking scenes commenced, it was obvious that Griffith did not have an adequate or appropriate voice for the role. The sequences were scrapped. In addition, she was to sing three songs, "Cliffs of Dover" at the embassy in Naples, "All Our Lovers" at the Palace in Palermo, and "Loch Lomond" at Vauxhall Gardens in London. There is a rather heart-hearted effort to synchronize the last, with new words by Francis Powers, to Corinne Griffith's lips, suggesting that she is singing. The record is silent as to the truth, but it seems unlikely that the star did her own singing; her approach to the lyrics of a song would have been as mediocre as her ability to mouth dialogue. She is certainly not playing the harp, although her fingering is accurate.

As the film's opening title explains, "This is the historic tale of two people whose lives are an immortal romance — the story of the love and destiny of England's greatest beauty, and England's greatest sailor."

The former is first seen when her mother, Mrs. Hart, arrives at the home of the Honorable Charles Greville. He is horrified by the behavior of her daughter, Emma, whom he describes as "a brazen hussy," but his friend, painter George Romney, persuades him to take the pair in, particularly as Emma assures him that she knows she is vulgar but could learn "from an elegant gentleman like you." The opening scenes move speedily along, diminished only by the over-the-top performance of Marie Dressler, who appears to think she is in a 19th century burlesque production rather than a major 20th century movie. She "chooses to make the most of her avoirdupois during certain junctures," commented Mordaunt

Frank Lloyd, seated next to Corinne Griffith, explains a scene set in Vauxhall Gardens for The Divine Lady.

Hall in the *New York Times* (March 23, 1929). That is a polite way of describing the extraordinary pantomime on display.

It is worth noting that early Warner Bros. correspondence refers to Mrs. Hart being played by Louise Dressler. Could it be that the studio really meant to hire Louise Dresser, equally overweight but far more talented, as her performance in the 1925 production of *The Goose Woman* illustrates?

Victor Varconi as Lord Nelson, Helen Jerome Eddy as his wife, and Evelyn Hall as the Duchess of Devonshire in The Divine Lady.

Greville takes Emma to the popular London amusement park, Vauxhall Gardens, and there, she meets Sir William Hamilton, who persuades Greville to send Emma and her mother to Naples, where he is British Ambassador. It is, in a way, a plot to have Emma marry Hamilton, a plot which misfires when she meets a visiting naval officer, Captain Horatio Nelson. Not only does Emma win over Nelson, she also persuades the King and Queen of Naples to permit Nelson's ship to take on provisions, in defiance of France. Here, for the first time, does the film hint at Emma's patriotism. It is influenced by her love for Nelson — but it is there, strong and clear. "You have saved England — and my honor, Lady Hamilton," he tells her. Again, after Nelson has disposed of the French fleet off the coast of Egypt, she is told, "England will always be grateful to you."

Sea battles and love scenes intercut, until Nelson's return to London. He rides in procession with Emma, while Sir William rides alone. At the Duchess of Devonshire's ball to honor Nelson, Emma is not invited, her place taken by Lady Nelson. When it is pointed out to Sir William that the Queen, who is also invited to the ball, has refused to acknowledge his wife, the ever-passive husband responds, "Her Majesty shows admirable discretion." As a result of the snob, Nelson takes Emma away to the country, to "find peace in our love."

It is in the security of a country home that Nelson is visited by Captain Hardy, begging him to return to his career as a naval officer and defend the English Channel against Napoleon. It is Emma who gives her consent to Nelson's return to duty: "England's won." It is the duality of the relationship that is here most obvious. Emma is secondly Nelson's mistress. Firstly, she is an Englishwoman, a patriot, who know where her duty lies as much as Nelson ultimately knows what he must do.

The film concludes with a major sea battle, with all the classic elements linked to Nelson: the signal to the fleet that "England expects that every man will do his duty" and, of course, the famous line, as Nelson lies dying, "Kiss me, Hardy." The film ends on a juxtaposition of shots, Nelson kissing Emma and then Hardy kneeling by his side as the hero dies. It would have been all Nelson, Hardy and ships at war, except that Lloyd chooses to cut away at one point to Emma's receiving what is to be her last letter from Nelson in which he assures her, "My thoughts are ever with you."

The film very much belongs to its star — and have no doubt that there is but one. "One could boil it down simply to the fact that Corinne Griffith gives a magnificent characterization," wrote the trade paper *Motion Picture News* (February 9, 1929). English-born H.B. Warner is true to his roots on the British stage in his role as Sir William Hamilton playing it with dignity and a sense of a man accepting of his position as the cuckolded husband of the mistress of a national hero. He had already played Jesus Christ in Cecil B. DeMille's 1927 production of *The King of Kings* and so stoicism and quiet anguish came naturally to him. The casting of Lord Nelson might seem odd in that the role went not to an Englishman but to a Hungarian, Victor Varconi. Some wondered why Clive Brook, in Hollywood at the time, was not the director's choice, but if Varconi was six inches taller than Nelson's five feet, six inches, he was still handsome enough to woo not only Lady Hamilton but also all the women in the audience. He was somewhat burly and forced to lose fifteen pounds on a grapefruit diet.

The actor did have some problems with remembering that his character had lost an arm, and that the costume hid his own limb. In his autobiography, he recalled,

"As the scene plays to a conclusion, the crippled Nelson leads his lady to the door, opens it and sadly watches as she goes out of his life forever.

"Frank Lloyd called for a cut.

"'Vic, I'm amazed,' Lloyd said.

"Had the scene gone that well?

"'I've studied Nelson for quite a time in preparation for this film. I know his battles, his life, his dislikes. But in this scene you've shown me something about the man I've never known. It's incredible.'

"My God, it must have been genius.

"'You see,' Lloyd continued, 'I knew Nelson had only one good eye but I never knew he had *three* arms.'

"In his exuberance, Victor had unthinkingly lifted his cramped arm out of the back harness and grandly swept the door open for his lady love. The result showed a right arm, a dangling sleeve and a sturdy third appendage growing out of his back and holding the door latch."[20]

The world premiere of *The Divine Lady* took place at the Carthay Circle Theatre in Los Angeles on January 29, 1929, hosted by director Fred Niblo. It was not a total critical success. Many reviewers complained that the sea battles were too many and too long. "One naval encounter is enough for any picture" was the reaction of *Photoplay* (March 1929). Objecting that the second sea battle was anti-climactic and that the Battle of Trafalgar lacked drama, *Motion Picture Classic* (June 1929) suggested that the film was "burdened with a story which never convinces aside from its romantic interludes." For Mordaunt Hall in the *New York Times* (March 23, 1929), "Frank Lloyd had the men, the money and the ships, but the development of some of his episodes is frequently abrupt and other scenes are marred by the new inevitable theme song." It was, nonetheless, "an ambitious and handsome production, one that frequently causes its failings to be pardoned."

Other critics had questions as to *The Divine Lady*'s historical accuracy. Writing in *Liberty* (November 10, 1928), Frederick James Smith complained that Emma's affairs with various men were "sugar-coated." Describing the production as "long and dreary," Smith comented, "As far as the celluloid Divine Lady is concerned, Emma is a beautiful young woman having a whole series of platonic affairs." More kindly was *Screen Secrets* (May 1929), stating the the film was "written with a whitewash brush and pictured with an artist's."

There was some positive commentary. In the *Los Angeles Evening Herald* (January 30, 1929), Harrison Carroll noted that the film "evidences the virility of Frank Lloyd's past efforts in the most spectacular sea fights ever screened. But on the whole it presents Lloyd in an entirely different mood — the creator of beautiful pictures." To Edwin Schallert in the *Los Angeles Times* (January 30, 1929), *The Divine Lady* was "lovely beyond compare in its embellishments of setting and costume."

The Divine Lady was well received in the United Kingdom, with Victor Varconi's attending the premiere in London. Happily, he was persuaded to keep his speech on stage after the film to two words, "Thank you," which he delivered in perfect, if softly spoken, English.

The Divine Lady won its director his first Academy Award. While, officially, there were no nominations published, Lloyd was actually in consideration for three films, *The Divine Lady, Drag* and *Weary River*.

There was a remake of sorts in 1940 when producer Alexander Korda made a film, titled, on its 1941 release, as *Lady Hamilton* in the United Kingdom, and *That Hamilton Woman* in the United States. Vivien Leigh and Laurence Olivier were starred in a film that was closer to reality, opening and closing with Emma Hamilton living in poverty in Calais, as happened after Nelson's death and the ending of *The Divine Lady*.[21] Just as with its predecessor, *That Hamilton Woman* emphasized patriotism but with somewhat more necessity in view of its being released prior to America's entry into World War Two. Frank Lloyd gave no published opinion of the film, but I am sure he would have approved.

1. "Imitation in the Film Game," New York Times, June 3, 1923, p. X2.

2. "Frank Lloyd Series for First National," The Moving Picture World, June 9, 1923, p. 511.

3. "Frank Lloyd Signed by First National," The Moving Picture World, April 21, 1923, p. 814.

4. Quoted in Kevin Brownlow, The Parade's Gone By, p. 368. It is comments such as this that have obviously served to hurt Lloyd's reputation in film history.

5. "Huge Location Camp for 'Sea Hawk,'" Motion Picture News, February 16, 1924, p. 735.

6. Photoplay, May 1924, p. 43.

7. Anthony Slide conversation with Isabel Falck, April 12, 2009.

8. "Four Lloyd Pictures for First National," The Moving Picture World, January 24, 1925, p. 381.

9. Motion Picture News, April 4, 1925, p. 1412. Aside from the Joseph Schenck productions, those of Frank Lloyd had the highest budgets.

10. Quoted in David Stenn, Clara Bow: Running Wild, p. 39.

11. Information from the Warner Bros. Archives, University of Southern California.

12. James Wingate to Hettie Gray Baker, October 14, 1933, Production Code Administration file on Hoop-La, Margaret Herrick Library, Academy of Motion Picture Arts and Sciences.

13. Agreement dated January 3, 1928, Warner Bros. Archives, University of Southern California.

14. Harry Carr, "A Wicked Lady," Screen Secrets, February 1929, p. 31.

15. Richard A. Rowland to W.R. Rothacker, January 13, 1928, Warner Bros. Archives, University of Southern California.

16. Fred Pelton to Al Rockett, June 27, 1928, Warner Bros. Archives, University of Southern California.

17. Al Rockett to Richard A. Rowland, June 28, 1928, Warner Bros. Archives, University of Southern California.

18. The State Insane Hospital is the same as the Los Angeles County Hospital; it was here, many years later, that Bela Lugosi was committed.

19. All quotes from Robert Parish, Growing up in Hollywood, pp. 54, 56, 57, 58.

20. Victor Varconi and Ed Honeck, It's Not Enough to Be Hungarian, pp. 108-109.

21. The opening and closing sequences were necessary in order for the film to comply with the Production Code, which could not permit a mistress to be rewarded for her behavior.

CHAPTER FOUR

From Silents to Sound

"We'd done just about all we could do with silent pictures," explained Frank Lloyd, reminiscing in 1936. "There weren't any new paths to trod and it was getting just a little bit boresome [sic]. Then when sound came in, I realized at once we couldn't handle it as they do on the stage. It had to be a merger between the old technique and the new.

"So I dug up the two best sound engineers in Hollywood, and for weeks I sat with them night and day, looking into the future, planning what courses to take. But only theoretically. I didn't want to learn too much about it…

"I want the road I set myself to be fairly wide, fairly clear. And anyway my job is directing — if I learn too much about how to record, and so forth, then I'll go sticking my nose into the soundman's affairs, which would be a hindrance to him and a waste of time for me.

"This business is a specialist's Paradise.

"I never studied camera either. Oh, I know the rudiments of photography. But that's a big job in itself and I don't want to confuse it with my interference. I get the best cameraman, the best soundman, and allow them full expression under certain control, of course. I tell the photographer what mood I want and let him find it; I tell the mixers what quality is needed and warn them about the spaces to leave for dubbing later. That's all. They do the rest, and I criticize when everything is finished. Usually the shots are perfect, the range for background music (I work with that department too) is just exactly right. And everybody is happy."[1]

In reality, Frank Lloyd ended his silent career on a high note with *Children of Divorce* and *The Divine Lady*, both illustrative of the high technical and emotional drama that might be accomplished in the medium. The former, released in April 1927 was the second of only two feature films produced by Lloyd under his so-called "long term" Paramount contract. The cast is headed by one of the studio's biggest stars, Clara Bow, whom Lloyd had directed in *Black Oxen*, supported by reliable and longstanding Paramount leading lady Esther Ralston, who had worked with the director on *Oliver Twist*, and up-and-coming Paramount star-to-be Gary Cooper.

Esther Ralston, Einar Hanson, Julia Swayne Gordon, and Norman Trevor in Children of Divorce.

As Kitty Flanders, Jean Waddington and Ted Larrabee respectively, they are the children of divorce of the title, dumped by their parents at a French convent, where they become friends. Still close in adulthood, Jean refuses to marry Ted until he gives up his profligate ways and becomes the engineer he had proposed, as a child, to become. Ultimately, however, it is Kitty who tricks Ted into marriage. Three years later, trapped in an unhappy relationship, she poisons herself and leaves her husband and her daughter to Jean.

Frank Lloyd's handling of the players and their roles could not be bettered. For those expecting a typically flamboyant and flirty performance, Clara Bow is a revelation here, allowed to mature into the sorrowful creature her character becomes. Esther Ralston quietly underplays throughout. Gary Cooper gives strong indication of the major star he is to become, and Lloyd titillates his female audience by having the actor, seen nude from the waist up, take a shower on camera.

The director understands how to bring out the emotion the characters are feeling by moving his camera (the cinematographer is Victor Milner) in close whenever necessary, and most pointedly to a close-up of Clara Bow's eyes, mirroring the unhappiness her character feels. He uses the

Frank Lloyd, below camera, directs a scene for Children of Divorce *with Gary Cooper, Clara Bow, Esther Ralston, and Einar Hanson.*

reverse effect when necessary as, for example, when the Clara Bow character has decided to take the poison and she walks away from the camera through two doors as it, in turn, moves away from her. Always, it is camera movement accentuating the drama of the moment, but never is the direction obvious.[2] As Mordaunt Hall wrote in the *New York Times* (April 26, 1927), "Mr. Lloyd's direction reveals a penchant for originality without reaching too far for effects."

At the end of the 1920s, Lloyd's career was somewhat in a state of flux. In the summer of 1927, it was announced that he would direct the John Barrymore vehicle *Tempest* for producer Joseph M. Schenck and United Artists release. However, "because of differences over the treatment of the story, he resigned."[3] Next, it was announced that as of January 1, 1928, he would return to the Fox Film Corporation. He did return to Fox, but not until the 1930s. Ultimately, the director remained under contract to First National through March 1931. All his films for the distributor were to be advertised on the main titles as "A Frank Lloyd Production," and he was to receive a salary of $2,750.00 a week.

Frank Lloyd's first "real" talkies, as opposed to *The Divine Lady*, which featured only music and sound effects, all starred Richard Barthelmess (1895-1963). The latter was a very natural actor, sensitive and boyishly good-looking in his early films, who developed in the mid 1920s into a mature, handsome leading man, very American and unaffected. Barthelmess was discovered by actress Alla Nazimova in 1916, when she featured him in her production of *War Brides*. He came to stardom with D.W. Griffith, appearing in *The Girl Who Stayed at Home* (1919), *Broken Blossoms* (1919), *Scarlet Days* (1919), *The Idol Dancer* (1920), *The Love Flower* (1920), and *Way Down East* (1920). Leaving Griffith, the actor consolidated his success with the title role in *Tol'Able David* in 1921. Arguably the screen's most popular male star, Barthelmess was under contract to First National, and so successful were his films with Frank Lloyd that an additional two-year contract was signed as of March 4, 1929. The contract gave the actor choice of stories, casts and directors. Happily, he had the good sense to select Lloyd in the last category. All the films were scripted by Bradley King, who was also responsible for the director's one non-Barthelmess talkie, *The Way of All Men*.

Richard Barthelmess and Frank Lloyd were good friends, and the former was a frequent guest at Lloyd's new home, to which he had moved around 1928. It was situated not in Beverly Hills or the wealthy Hancock Park area of Los Angeles, but in Whittier, a small city situated in the San Gabriel Valley, some twelve miles east of downtown Los Angeles.

The two men made their sound debuts with *Weary River*, shot late in 1928, based on a short story by Courtney Ryley Cooper, published in *Collier's Weekly*, and purchased by First National in August 1928 for $5,000.00. A sentimental gangster drama (if there can be such a contradictory type of subject), *Weary River* has the Barthelmess character sent "up the river" on a framed charge by an underworld rival. In prison, he becomes a radio singing star, performing with the prison orchestra. From sullen prisoner, he is transformed to warden's pet. The radioland audience loves the singer so much that it succeeds in forcing the Governor to grant him a pardon. The film served a dual purpose in proving that Barthelmess could talk and that his voice was pleasing and not inappropriate to his appearance, and, equally, that Lloyd was just as capable with a sound drama as a silent one. Mordaunt Hall in the *New York Times* (January

25, 1929) sarcastically pointed out that Barthelmess looked younger and healthier after a few years in prison.

Weary River is not a full talkie in that the sound sequences are interspersed between silent sections, accompanied by a recorded Vitaphone score. Today, audiences generally find such hybrid productions, moving from silent to sound and back again, as distracting. It was not so in 1929.

Richard Barthelmess and Betty Compson in Weary River.

Variety (January 30, 1929) praised the director for proving "that the 50-50 method of sandwiching talk between periods of silent relaxation is the best way of circumventing the nervous exhaustion which some of the all-talkers have occasioned, *Weary River* captures again that much-handled 'visual flow,' allegedly assassinated by conversation. It moves with well-lubricated serenity."

The film was produced at a time when theme songs were at their height, and *Weary River* does not disappoint with a title song, performed some four times: hopefully, spiritually, brokenly and, finally, as a symbol of redemption, in tune with the rehabilitation of the Barthelmess character. There was "as much 'Weary River' as one ever wants to hear" was Mordaunt Hall's opinion. With music by Louis Silvers and words by Grant Clarke, "Weary River" was derided by critics, thanks to its over-performance and the banality of its lyrics:

"*I have been just like a wea-ea-eary river*
"*That keeps wi-i-inding endlessly-y-y.*
"*Fate has been a very chee-ee-erful giver*
"*To most e-e-every one but me-e-e-e.*"

Initially, it was claimed that Richard Barthelmess was both singing and accompanying himself at the piano. Neither was true. It was quickly revealed that the voice "double" was Johnny Murray, a former cornetist at the Coconut Grove in Los Angeles, and the piano was played offstage by Frank Churchill.[4] Dubbing was not known at this stage, and would have been virtually impossible with the Vitaphone sound-on-disc process, and, thus, Murray and Churchill performed out of camera range, while Barthelmess, on camera mouthed the words and ran his unseen fingers over the unseen piano keyboard. Frank Churchill enjoyed a major career in later years, composing the songs for the Walt Disney productions of *Three Little Pigs*, *Dumbo*, *Snow White and the Seven Dwarfs*, and *Bambi*.

It would be foolish to suggest that *Weary River* is a great film or in any way comparable to earlier efforts by both its star and director. At best, it can be described, in the words of Richard Watts, Jr., writing in the New York *Tribune* (January 25, 1929), as "unpretentious, entertaining, somewhat didactic melodrama." However, thanks to *Weary River*, "Barthelmess is the first full-fledged silent star to meet the menacing talkie and emerge a bigger player," wrote Frederick James Smith in *Liberty* (March 9, 1929).

Weary River was the subject of a 1938 uncredited remake by Warner Bros., titled *Over the Wall*, directed by Frank MacDonald, and with Dick Foran as the singing convict, who this time around is not dubbed.

When the next Barthelmess-Lloyd production, *Drag*, was released in July 1929, at least one critic had to point out that it had no connection to the notorious Mae West stage production of the same title. There is no cross dressing in *Drag*, but rather an ordinary young man, with ambitions, who is dragged down by his wife's family. The film was well received by the critics, with Creighton Peet in the *New York Evening Post* (June 21,

Richard Barthelmess and Marion Nixon in Young Nowheres.

1929) describing it as "a faithful, intelligent and on the whole convincing drama with a [sic] idea." In *Judge*, noted leftist critic Pare Lorentz described *Drag* as "a movie with some breath of life…the simplicity and honesty of the story lift *Drag* out of the routine."

The best known of the Barthelmess-Lloyd efforts is *Weary River*, but the best is, unquestionably, the little known *Young Nowheres*, which is very reminiscent of the 1928 silent film by Paul Fejos, *Lonesome*. The star is a wistful hero, possessing some of the qualities he had shown almost a decade earlier in *Tol'able David*. Here, Barthelmess, playing younger than his age and doing it well, is Albert "Binky" Whelan, an elevator boy at New York's Creighton Apartments. He faces a night court judge, accused of harboring a young girl, Annie Jackson, played by Marion Nixon, in the apartment of Mr. Cleaver. As he tells the story to the judge, Whelan explains that he and his girl have no place to go to be alone. When he learns that the Cleaver apartment will be empty over Christmas, he takes Annie, who is suffering from pneumonia, there. Cleaver returns unexpectedly and accuses Whelan of using his apartment for immoral purposes. After listening to Whelan's story, he refuses to press charges and the judge is happy to dismiss the case.

The title comes from a remark made by the film's philosophical drunk, Mr. Jesse, played by Bert Roach, a gentleman who promises to take care of the couple after the court case is dismissed. He describes the pair as having "come from nothing and going nowheres."

Unlike *Lonesome*, which was shot in New York and used Coney Island as a major backdrop, *Young Nowheres* was filmed entirely in Los Angeles and at the Burbank Studios of First National. The Coney Island set was assembled on a six-acre studio lot, built in two weeks by a reported eighty-five workmen. There was some night filming at Ocean Park, Santa Monica, with Busch Gardens, Pasadena, standing in for Central Park.

The film was highly praised, with *Screenland* (December 1929) describing it as "an honest, sincere and courageous drama." Writing in the *New York Herald-Tribune* (October 2, 1929), Richard Watts, Jr. commented that *Young Nowheres* "substitutes gentleness for gunplay, sweetness for a theme song, and simplicity for a murder case…Into the story, however, the director…has managed to put something of compassion and understanding for two helpless, beaten humans." With perhaps the highest praise possible, *Photoplay* (December 1929) wrote, "If there is today a successor to the simplicity of [D.W.] Griffith, it is Frank Lloyd." It is a telling comment indicative of Lloyd's ability to handle simple scenes as well as the spectacular and crowd sequences for which he was generally praised.

The Barthelmess of the next Lloyd production *Son of the Gods*, is a throwback to his characterization of the gentle Chinese hero in *Broken Blossoms*. The film is also unfortunately reminiscent of Lloyd's *A Tale of Two Worlds*. Like *Broken Blossoms*, *Son of the Gods* shows the ill treatment of the Chinese by the white races and pleads for racial understanding and tolerance. It does it in wildly melodramatic fashion with a trite storyline from an original by Rex Beach.

The Barthelmess character is brought up by a wealthy Chinese nobleman and falls in love with the heroine, played by Constance Bennett. When she discovers he is Chinese, she horsewhips the poor guy. However, the pair are reunited at the end when it is revealed that the Barthelmess character is really a white man.

Receiving the most praise were Barthelmess' speaking some Chinese, along with a handful of Technicolor sequences. Writing in *Picture*

Play (May 1930), Norbert Lusk described the film as "well directed and handsomely produced." But most reviews echoed the comments of Mordaunt Hall in the *New York Times* (January 31, 1930), who noted that it "plods its way through banal episodes until the final happy fade-out."

Barthelmess returned again to his Griffith years, with *The Lash*, reminiscent of *Scarlet Days*. In this bandit story, with the working title and initial release title of *Adios*, set in New Mexico and California of 1846, Barthelmess plays El Puma with Mary Astor as his sweetheart. Marion Nixon is featured, but as the star's sister rather than the love interest. Lloyd shot the film at the studio and on location in Calabasas to the north of Los Angeles. "So slow-paced it almost stands still" was the opinion of *Motion Picture Magazine* (January 1930).

Mary Astor is not particularly kind about her co-star:

"*The Lash* was probably one of the weakest picture he ever did, and he was no longer young enough to play a dashing Robin Hood bandit. He was a short, stocky man, and had to wear a girdle to pull in a slight paunch, and he used to cuss because it made him 'short of breath,' when what he was really cussing about was the inevitable encroachment of middle age."[5]

Despite the girdle, Richard Barthelmess continued on screen through 1942 — and briefly reunited with Frank Lloyd for a featured role in *The Spoilers*. The five films that the two made together in a period of little over a year are not great productions, but neither should they be dismissed as unimportant in the careers of either man. They kept Richard Barthelmess at the top of his profession, and helped Frank Lloyd to come to terms with the sound motion picture, to learn its possibilities, and to improve as a director in the new medium.

After finishing with Barthelmess, Lloyd was loaned by First National to Fox as of August 4, 1930, to direct *East Lynne*, and to Howard Hughes' The Caddo Co. in February 1931 to direct *The Age for Love*, starring Billie Dove. First National received $3,000.00 per week for ten weeks of Lloyd's services as Howard Hughes' director.[6]

---

1. Quoted in Howard Sharpe, "The Star Creators of Hollywood: Frank Lloyd," p. 104.

2. Josef von Sternberg was an assistant director at Paramount at the time, and he claims in his autobiography, Fun in a Chinese Laundry, that he remade half of the film. There is no proof of Sternberg's claim, and it is difficult to believe that an assistant director would have been called in to redo the work of a major studio director.

3. The Moving Picture World, September 17, 1927, p. 159.

4. There were early reports that Barthelmess was voice "doubled" by Frank Withers, but these proved to be incorrect.

5. Mary Astor, A Life on Film, New York: Delacorte Press, 1971, p. 87.

6. Information taken from the Warner Bros. Archives, University of Southern California.

CHAPTER FIVE

Cavalcade and the British Image

Frank Lloyd was as sympathetic to British themes as he was to seafaring ones. They are the two types of productions that predominate in the director's canon of films. While no one could question Lloyd's loyalty to his adopted country, just as he loved the sea, he also loved Britain and the British way of life. He had a natural affinity to the country that gave him birth and where he had grown up. With these two types of melodramas Lloyd is at his most assured best.

Who is more representative of British womanhood than Diana Wynyard? And who most exemplifies the stiff upper lip British male than Clive Brook? They are the British upper class personified: strong, dignified, devoid of unnecessary emotion, and, if perhaps not ready to wave the flag, at the least ready to clarify what is stands for. The British working classes are, perhaps, less clearly defined. Una O'Connor might seem to be the overly dramatic representative of her class, but she is, of course, Irish and not English. Herbert Mundin was born in the English county of Lancashire and is very much the Lancashire Lad, a mix of servility and comic arrogance. He was certainly a favorite of Frank Lloyd, featured in *Cavalcade*, *Hoopla*, *Mutiny on the Bounty*, and *Under Two Flags* — and might probably have turned up in some later productions had he not been killed in a 1939 Los Angeles automobile accident.

The British community are not well represented in Lloyd's silent films, but they are prominent in his sound features, and include Beryl Mercer (*East Lynne* and *Berkeley Square*), Leslie Howard and Heather Angel (*Berkeley Square*), Charles Laughton (*Mutiny on the Bounty*), Ronald Colman (*Under Two Flags* and *If I Were King*), Basil Rathbone, Henry Wilcoxon and Heather Thatcher (*If I Were King*), Margaret Lockwood and Will Fyffe (*Rulers of the Sea*), Sir Cedric Hardwicke (*The Howards of Virginia*), and most of the cast of *Cavalcade*. Irene Browne and Valerie Taylor came from the stage to appear in *Berkeley Square*.

All of Lloyd's "British" films were produced at Fox, the first, *East Lynne*, on loan out from First National. The first sound version with the original title of the classic melodrama of stage and the printed page seems a natural for Frank Lloyd. *East Lynne* is possibly the most famous melodrama in

The top four director at Fox in the early 1930s are, left to right, Frank Lloyd, Henry King, John Ford, and Frank Borzage.

history, written in 1861 by Mrs. Henry Wood. Her novel was dramatized for the stage, initially as a five act drama and, in the early 20th century, as a three act drama for American audiences by Ned Albert. The story gave to the English language a much-quoted line, delivered by Lady Isabel Vane, when she realizes that the son she has abandoned has succumbed without recognizing her: "Dead! And never called me mother!" It is actually a line that appears neither in the original novel nor in the more recent American stage adaptation. The story also gives rise to much amusement with English audiences in that Lady Isabel's son is named "Little Willie," unfortunate in that "willie" is a popular slang term for penis.

East Lynne was much filmed, at least up to Lloyd's version. In the United Kingdom, it was first presented on screen in 1902 in a half-reel presentation in five scenes, with Mrs. A.W. Fitzgerald as the leading lady.

By 1910, the reels had increased to one-and-a-half for a new adaptation by the Precision Company. A 1913 production was two reels in length, with Nell Emerald and H. Agar Lyons as the stars. In 1922, Harry B. Parkinson produced a one-reel adaptation for his series, "Tense Moments with Great Authors," starring Iris Hoey. The most prominent British version was a six-reel adaptation by Barker in 1913, starring Blanche Forsythe and Fred Paul, which was released in the United States by the Box Office Attraction Film Rental Co.

The earliest American version was Vitagraph's 1909 one-reeler, *East Lynne; or, Led Astray*. In 1912, Thanhouser produced a two-reel version starring Florence LaBadie. Three years later, the American Biograph Company made a three-reel version, with Louise Vale. In 1916, Theda Bara and Stuart Holmes starred in a five-reel adaptation for Fox. Mabel Ballin and Edward Earle were the stars of a seven-reel version in 1921 from Hugo Ballin Productions. The last silent version, in 1925, was again from Fox with Alma Rubens and Edmund Lowe starring, under Emmett Flynn's direction. Almost simultaneous with filming of the Frank Lloyd version, Liberty Productions released the first sound production of *East Lynne* under the title of *Ex-Flame*. The storyline, written by the film's director Victor Halperin, was much changed and even the central character, played by Marion Nixon, was retitled Lady Catherine.

In 1931, British director George Pearson made *East Lynne on the Western Front*, in which the play is burlesqued by soldiers in France in 1915. The role of Lady Isobel is played by later Frank Lloyd favorite, Herbert Mundin.

"Frank Lloyd's *East Lynne*," as the main title card describes it, began shooting in November 1930 for a March 1931 release. The basic storyline follows the novel as Lady Isobel Dane (Ann Harding) marries lawyer Robert Carlisle (Conrad Nagel) despite an obvious attraction to Captain Francis Levison (Clive Brook). Carlisle takes his new bride to his country home of East Lynne, which is dominated by his sister Cornelia (Cecelia Loftus). Separated from her London friends, Isobel becomes lonely and frustrated despite giving birth to a son, William. When she allows Levison to escort her to a county ball, Cornelia lies about the relationship to her brother, Isobel leaves East Lynne, forbidden to take her son with her, and she and her husband are divorced. Moving to the continent, Isobel takes up with Levison, who is something of a cad. Eventually, Isobel returns to East Lynne to see her son one last time.

One prominent difference between the novel and the film is that Lloyd introduces the Franco-Prussian War into the proceedings, allowing for some major crowd scenes not only in Vienna but also in besieged Paris.

The major change is in the ending. In Paris, during the siege, Isobel is knocked unconscious as the building behind her is hit by a shell. Recovering, she learns that her optic nerve has been severed and that at any moment she will go blind. She returns secretly to East Lynne, where faithful nurse Joyce (Beryl Mercer) allows her to see and spend the night with her son. In the morning, Isobel is blind. Carlyle discovers her presence, orders her to leave and fires Joyce, who takes the opportunity to expose Cornelia as the source of the breakup of the marriage. Isobel wanders from the home with Carlyle in pursuit. She falls to her death into a convenient ravine, and Carlyle carries her body back to East Lynne. And so, it is the mother rather than the son whose tragic death concludes the story.

One can only wonder at Isobel's choosing Carlyle over Levison. Clive Brook as the latter has style, not to mention a better vocal delivery, while Conrad Nagel is his usual wooden self. Levison promises "happiness always" to Isobel at her wedding, but the shot at the end of the scene of his pensive facial expression suggests it is not to be. That same thought is continued with the first shot of Cornelia, whose ominous presence at East Lynne, is emphasized as the camera moves in from a considerable distance to a closer shot as she stands at the foot of the stairs. It is the first of many such moving camera shots in the film, each emphasizing mood. When the camera is moving, there is generally silence, and director Lloyd tends often to rely on menacing moments of quiet and even entire silent sequences.

From the start, it is obvious that Cornelia is the controlling influence at East Lynne. Her comments are designed to make Isobel feel uncomfortable, while her husband's comparison of her to his mother does not help. "I love to be flattered. And I love to be happy," says Isobel, but at East Lynne she will be neither. Only Joyce offers comfort, telling her that the house had been "so full of twilight" prior to Isobel's coming.

The pacing is slow, and yet three years pass with remarkable speed as Isobel settles down to life at East Lynne and bears her husband an heir.

Once Isobel and Levison are reunited in Vienna, it is obvious that the former is not accepted in respectable society, while her lover is revealed as someone who has gambled with his career, "rotten and weak underneath." After the couple move to Paris, it is Levison who demands fiscal responsibility from Isobel, suggesting she order a cheaper wine than champagne. In one of the best lines of the film, the lady responds, "Please, let's not get common."

After the accident, Isobel wanders through the Paris crowds, part of them but not of them. In many ways, the scene is similar to Diana Wynyard's wandering through the crowds in London celebrating the Armistice.

Once she had determined to return to East Lynne, the ending is obvious. "His face is the last thing I will ever see," Isobel tells Joyce in regard to her son, of whose growth she has been kept aware thanks to secret letters from the latter. As a result of Carlyle's initially throwing her out of the house, the final big speech in the film is left to Beryl Mercer as Joyce. Although not always a satisfactory actress, Mercer carries off the scene reasonably well.

Frank Lloyd with Bradley King on his arm accompanies co-writer Tom Barry to lunch while shooting East Lynne.

But then she does not have too much competition from Conrad Nagel.

It has been suggested that Frank Lloyd's Scottish reserve helps control the bathos of Mrs. Henry Wood, and there is some truth to this. The melodrama never gets out of hand thanks to some major non-intimate sequences and the measured acting from Ann Harding and Clive Brook. The situation in which they find themselves is not as forced as one might imagine. Even Isobel's loss of her son to his father is not overplayed or over-dramatized.

The studio had high hopes for the production, describing it as a "Super-Special," and requiring exhibitors to book it on a separate basis from the regular Fox output. It was nominated for the Academy Award for Best Picture, but lost out to *Cimarron*, which is about as heavy-handed a production as it is possible to make.

From a modern perspective, *East Lynne*, the film, is almost as dated as *East Lynne*, the novel — and neither superior nor inferior to *Cimarron*. Surprisingly, contemporary reviewers were effusive in their praise. The trade paper *Motion Picture Herald* (February 28, 1931) commented,

"This may be called, from the dramatic standpoint, one of the finest films of the year. From the production angle, it comes very near to being a perfect piece of work. Naturally enough, it has appeal, more appeal, and then some more all the way through. It is the sort of thing that audiences go for in a really big way. There is plenty of evidence that expense has not been spared in its making.

"The picture is a natural effective and tear inciting piece of film work. Even the most self-contained person viewing it will undoubtedly be moved to sympathy, which may take its toll in slight weeping. It is a picture for the family and for everyone."

Even the usually sedate and reality grounded Mordaunt Hall in the *New York Times* (February 21, 1931) was enthused when the film opened in New York at the Roxy Theatre. "Frank Lloyd's direction…is vastly superior to anything he has done in several years," he wrote. "The play does not seem so very old as it is done here."

East Lynne was followed by a minor piece, *Passport to Hell*, written by Leon Gordon and Lloyd's faithful screenwriter Bradley King. There is a something of a British theme in that the story concerns an English woman, played by Elissa Landi, who is trapped in German West Africa as World War One breaks out. There, she is protected by the son of the German commandant, played by Paul Lukas, whom the woman marries. Aside from its English connection, the film also features a steamer ship and was filmed in part at a favorite Frank Lloyd location, Santa Catalina Island (standing in for German West Africa). All the Frank Lloyd elements are there.

Production values are high, and the acting is strong, although Elissa Landi always gives the appearance of slight characterization, much too timid and restrained. The story is by novelist Harry Hervey, best remembered for *Shanghai Express*, but it is the plot that was generally criticized at the time. When the film opened at New York's Winter Garden Theatre on August 26, 1932, it was viewed by *New York Times* critic Mordaunt Hall, who complained that it lacked both dramatic strength and clever dialogue. In other words, the plot is formulaic.

As Noel Coward recalled, "I had dashed off *Cavalcade* in a few days."[1] It was the most spectacular of any of Coward's writings and was intended to provide Charles B. Cochran with a new production for London's Theatre Royal, Drury Lane, a show that would be entirely British in concept and staging and stand up to any threat of a "Broadway invasion" of the London theatre scene. *Cavalcade* was a slice of British history, covering the period 1899 through 1929, seen from the viewpoint of an upper middle class London family and their servants. It was the upstairs/downstairs lives of the Marryots and the Bridges. It is a patriotic saga of the British Empire, but, also, a tragedy, as each family, particularly the Marryots, lose loved ones. The staging of the play required a cast and crew of three hundred, and yet the playscript is relatively short in that dialogue is kept to a minimum and largely simplistic, with music as important as dialogue.

Cavalcade opened on October 13, 1931, and ran for 405 performances. The film rights were acquired fairly late in the run by the Fox Film Corporation. As Noel Coward recalled, an American lady named Mrs. Tinker was so impressed by the play that she cabled her husband urging him to acquire the rights. Mr. Tinker was Edward Richmond Tinker, a distinguished banker who in November 1931 had become president of the Fox Film Corporation. Over the objections of his colleagues at the studio, Tinker prevailed in persuading the company to acquire the rights. Coward claimed that the studio had little interest in the project, that they hired "Frank Lloyd, who I believe had been wandering unemployed through the Hollywood limbo for some," and then, "washed their hands of the whole affair." Coward maintained the lack of studio interest "enabled Frank Lloyd, who was a brilliant director, to carry on with his job without indeed much encouragement but also without interference."[2]

There may be some truth to what Coward remembers, but, in reality, Fox was very enthused about the project. The studio paid Coward $100,000.00 for the rights, including the use of his music. Frank Borzage, who had known Frank Lloyd since their time together as actors at Universal, was assigned to shoot an afternoon performance of the play for reference and casting purposes, although it is somewhat unclear what direction would be needed in filming a stage production as performed. Perhaps, Fox had in mind that Borzage would be the director of the screen adaptation. He was certainly under contract to the studio at this time, and in May 1932 he was under the illusion that he was to work with Noel Coward on the production. However, a month later, he was loaned out to Paramount to direct *A Farewell to Arms*, and the reality is that Borzage had never directed anything as ambitious in terms of its scope or magnitude as *Cavalcade*.

The Production Code Administration, Hollywood's self-censoring authority, was extremely enthused about the production, and spent considerable time in correspondence with Fox and others. As far as the Code's

Jason S. Joy was concerned, it was the general belief "that it is one of the outstandpoint [sic] possibilities of all time."[3] Joy was concerned with Fox's plans "to make [the film] more acceptable for American audiences."[4] The advice of Dr. Alington, headmaster of the prestigious British public school, Eton, was sought by the Production Code Administration. He was not totally positive, commenting,

Frank Lloyd on the set of Cavalcade *with Bonita Granville, Ursula Jeans and Una O'Connor.*

"I thought it was superb as a spectacle and in many parts most moving, but it was completely spoilt for me by the fact that the author did not appear to have any real remedy for the troubles of the world. It is all very well for the father and mother to drink to its future prosperity in a holy manner at the end, but what singular constructive idea have they suggested, particularly to their children."

Fox production chief Winfield Sheehan analyzed the film of the play, noting the audience response to its comic lines, rating them as "a laugh," "a good laugh" or "terrific laugh." "We must avoid sophistication or subtlety," he wrote to Frank Lloyd. "We must be plain and not miss any theatrical trick that will give entertainment or emotional effect upon the audience."[5] Sheehan noted that the stage play had used an electric signboard on the proscenium arch to indicate the year of each episode, and that it was important to use titles to fix the period and year in the film. He advocated the use of popular songs, as Coward had done, and suggested the addition of "Oh, You Beautiful Doll," the rights to which were owned by the studio. He urged that it be produced in such a way that once Bridges, the butler, had returned from the Boer War, he be shown as "a rum-soaked, red-nosed Bolshevik maniac from alcohol... He is the symbol of the curse of hard liquor and the curse of money and better position." Sheehan was quite concerned that the film be a tract against Bolshevism. In all, Sheehan devoted twelve pages to his ideas and analysis.

From the original stage production, Fox hired Una O'Connor (Ellen Bridges), Merle Tottenham (Annie) and Irene Browne (Margaret Harris). Curiously, the studio ignored one film-star-to-be in the cast, John Mills (Joe Marryot), and while it did hire Binnie Barnes (Fanny Bridges), she subsequently decided not to play the role being dissatisfied with the manner in which it had been adapted for the screen. Why she should have had any objections is not clear. The two central characters of Robert and Jane Maryot were played on the London stage by Edward Sinclair and Mary Clare. They were replaced in the film by Clive Brook and Diana Wynyard. Noel Coward described the latter's performance as "sincere and beautiful...as I had hoped to see in the picturisation of my play. I think I shall always see her standing in Trafalgar Square or saying goodbye to the last of her sons at the station. Yes, Jane-Diana-Marryot-Wynyard will always live for me, as I am sure she will for all those who go to see *Cavalcade*."[6]

With heavy pre-production activity, primarily involving the building of mammoth sets and creation of period costumes, actual filming on *Cavalcade* was completed in a couple of months, October through November

1932. All the sets were constructed at what was then known as Movietone City in Westwood and is now the 20th Century Fox studio. According to the pressbook, where exaggeration would be the norm, the film boasts forty principal parts, 150 speaking parts, more than 2,500 actors in one scene, 15,000 minor characters, and 25,000 costumes. Produced at a cost of $1,300,000.00, *Cavalcade* grossed in excess of $3,500,000.00.

Diana Wynyard and Clive Brook as a young and worried-looking Jane and Robert Marryot in Cavalcade.

Noel Coward was in Hollywood at least for part of the pre-production, attending what was described as the first technical conference. He had complained that he managed to recognize "a few of his original lines"[7] in the Paramount production of *Tonight Is Ours*, released simultaneous with *Cavalcade* and based on his 1926 play *The Queen Was in the Parlor*. He could not have made the same complaint about *Cavalcade*, whose script by Britisher Reginald Berkeley closely follows the original.

Both open on New Year's Eve, 1899, as Robert and Jane Marryot toast the new century with their children, Joey and Edward, and their servants Ellen and Alfred Bridges. The two men are to leave the next day to fight in the Boer War. After their return, Alfred Bridges leaves to take over a pub, where his mother-in-law Mrs. Snapper will join Ellen and their daughter Fanny. However, prior to leaving the Marryot household, the servants and their employers gather on the balcony for Queen Victoria's funeral; a funeral presented without a single shot of the actual procession.

When Jane and son Edward visit the Bridges, they find that Alfred has become an abusive alcoholic. He throws a doll that Jane had brought for Fanny into the fire; the girl runs out into the street, and when Alfred goes after her, he is killed by a fire truck. Jane meets Ellen and Fanny

A very posed photograph of Frank Lawton as Joey, the last of the Marryot sons to die in Cavalcade, *cheek to cheek with Diana Wynyard as his mother.*

again at the seashore in 1909, where Edward confesses his love for Edith, the daughter of family friend Margaret Harris. On April 14, 1912, the couple celebrate their honeymoon on an ocean liner, which is revealed to be the Titanic.

With the outbreak of World War One, against the wishes of his mother, Joey enlists. Later, he begins a love affair with Fanny Bridges, who is now a musical comedy star. On November 11, 1918, Ellen Bridges visits Jane to reveal the relationship between her daughter and the latter's son. She insists that the two must marry, but at this crucial moment, a telegram arrives, announcing that Joey has been killed.

Time passes. At a nightclub on New Year's Eve, 1932, Fanny sings the latest hit song, "Twentieth Century Blues." At the Marryot home, an elderly Robert and Jane drink a toast to the future.[8]

On the printed page, the plot, such as it is, reads stilted, simplistic and oddly contrived. It succeeds, as it had succeeded on the stage, thanks to the production values, the performances, the use of popular music for emotional effect — as Coward himself wrote, cheap music can be terribly potent — and because of the direction. The dialogue is really kept to a minimum — in fact the playscript is less than sixty printed pages complete — and, to a large extent, as some modern critics have observed, it is almost a silent film with musical effects. Here, as he had done in the past, Frank Lloyd demonstrates how he can handle crowds for dramatic impact, and, yet, at the same time, he is capable of getting every last emotion out of a simple scene. The most impressive of the spectacular sequences depicts the troopship about to leave for South Africa. Through a series of carefully orchestrated shots, Lloyd presents the scale of the outdoor set, with literally hundreds of extras and a ship's frontage that does not move but give the distinct impression to the audience that it is about to.

The "downstairs" characters are here primarily for comic relief. There is very obviously an aura of condescension in terms of how they are presented — very much as working class stereotypes. But the fault, if fault there be, must squarely be directed at Noel Coward.

Of course, Lloyd is helped by the dialogue and staging from the original production as with one of the most potent moments in the show when Edward and Edith are on their honeymoon and only, at the end of the scene, is it revealed that they are sailing on the doomed liner, *Titanic*. On stage, Edith removes her coat from the rail of the ship to show the lifeboat with its tragic name; on screen, the couple walk away to disclose the lifebelt which their bodies had hidden. The sense of shock and sorrow from the audience is enhanced by the playing on the soundtrack of "Nearer, My God, to Thee." The entire sequence is devoid of sophisticated cinematic techniques. There are just two camera angles, one of which is a reverse shot. It is simple and sincere.

One scene added to the film, of which Coward approved, was a meeting in France, during World War One, between Robert and Joey, father and son fighting a common foe, just as father and servant had fought in the Boer War. It is a brief and casual moment, with neither realizing that it is the last time they will be together.

Coward did not care for the shots of both men and women, in medieval attire riding across the screen with the passing of the years, and first seen under the main titles. Presumably, the notion was to present British history on the move. Far more impressive, and logical, is the montage of shots showing soldiers on the march and dying as World War One moves ruthlessly on from year to year. By all accounts, he did approve of a major reworking of the last scenes. On stage, the toast does not end the production, but is followed by a night club scene, with "Twentieth Century Blues" being performed. Downstage are Jane and Robert with their champagne glasses held aloft, while the music and noise grows louder and louder, only to be followed by darkness and silent. As the lights go up on the whole stage, the cast are seen standing in tiers in front of a Union Jack, while singing "God Save the King."

That was the order of scenes in the original outline treatment by Reginald Berkeley, dated July 22, 1932. The final shooting script of September 19, 1932 was different. The night club sequence is now the penultimate one in the movie, followed by that most moving of all toasts, delivered by Diana Wynyard as Jane Marryot:

"Now, then, let's couple the Future of England with the past of England. The glories and victories and triumphs that are over, and the sorrows that are over, too. Let's drink to our sons who made part of the pattern and to our hearts that died with them. Let's drink to the spirit of gallantry and courage that made a strange Heaven out of unbelievable Hell, and let's drink to the hope that one day this country of ours, which we love so much, will find dignity and greatness and peace again."

As the toast concludes, there are a series of montage shots depicting the madness, tragedy, speed, and politics of the present. The camera cuts back to the couple, with Clive Brook reprising the last line of the toast. The crowds in Trafalgar Square singing "Auld Lang Syne" (which has served as a musical motif throughout the film) is a logical conclusion, but, almost surprisingly, there is another cut to what is presumably St. Paul's Cathedral in silhouette and the playing of the British National Anthem. (Many American audiences perhaps did not realize that the music was so very British in that it is also the music to "My Country 'T is of Thee.")

Perhaps to Frank Lloyd himself, the most moving moment was the funeral of Queen Victoria — "she must have been a very little lady," says Joey — in that he had been there, as he recalled in old age:

"It began with another hush and other massed thousands. There was a boy's birthday on February 2, 1901, and I was that fourteen-year-old boy climbing up a wall, grabbing for an iron railing to hoist myself above the heads of the crowd. The London watchers were silent, seeing the last of the longest ruler in British history — Queen Victoria — and her funeral cortege with the nine monarchs following behind her coffin. No other royal spectacle has been as impressive, before or since.

"Beside me, an unwieldy box had a wooden crank which ground on. The operator ignored all questions as he cranked the odd contraption by hand. Nobody could tell me what the bulky machine was until a British bobby or policeman spoke low, 'That's called a Mutoscope. It makes the pictures wot move, lad. An' hang on tight to that railing afore you falls an' breaks yer bleedin' little neck.'

"I was to spend my mature years trying to make pictures which moved, but this was the first film camera I had seen."[9]

Two problems remained to be resolved. The first was the deletion required by the Production Code Administration of "The scene in the cabaret depicting twentieth century life, showing two young women seated together, one holding the other's hand, carrying a suggestion of sex perversion." The other was the use of the word "hell," banned under the Production Code, along with "damn" and "bloody." The words could not be cut as the actors were unavailable to reshoot. Eventually, Will Hays, head of the Production Code, agreed that "The sweep of the picture is such that they will probably pass unnoticed."[10]

Cavalcade received its world premiere in Hollywood at Grauman's Chinese Theatre on January 12, 1933, complete with a prologue providing a French version of the film and titled "Montmartre," beginning in the 18th Century and closing in 1933. Frank Lloyd was present with his wife, worried that this was "a story of another country," but believing that "emotions are never foreign but universal in their impact." As the film concluded with the British National Anthem, there was silence in the auditorium. Then the lights came up, and the audience stood and applauded. Will Rogers, master of ceremonies, came on stage, commenting, "Well, we've seen it and I don't know what you all think, but to me, it rang the bell." He continued, "A big movie is not the work of one man, but it is controlled and guided by one man," as he beckoned Lloyd to the stage.[11]

Even the leftist film critic Pare Lorentz, writing in *Vanity Fair* (March 1933) praised the film as "a superlative newsreel, forcibly strengthened by factual scenes, good music, and wonderful photography." He did, of course, criticize Noel Coward as a "choleric old empire-builder" and objected strongly to the film's concluding "sophomoric toast." A harsher criticism came from the *New York Herald Tribune* (January 29, 1933), "Mr. Coward has turned into a sort of moral Fascist…Like all other Fascists, political, religious or intellectual, he couches his new beliefs in terms far too simple to…carry even a modest burden of truth."

The Fox Film Corporation promptly signed Una O'Connor and Merle Tottenham to contracts. Herbert Mundin was already under contract to the studio, but, as a result of his work in *Cavalcade*, the renewal option was taken up early.

Frank Lloyd, the ex-pat, must have been very pleased to read in that venerable British newspaper, *The Times*, that "America is to be congratulated on having made the best film of English life that has ever been made." Other British newspapers, along with Noel Coward, were equally impressed. In *The Sunday Times* (February 19, 1933), Sydney W. Carroll described the production as "the noblest, most inspiring film concerned with the British people ever made in the world since pictures began. I shall make myself ridiculous were I to employ all the superlatives that come into my mind as I think of it." "*Cavalcade* is one of those rare pictures that give dignity and stature to the screen," wrote Campbell Dixon in *The Daily Telegraph* (February 20, 1933). In *The Observer* (February 19, 1933), C.A. Lejeune wrote, "*Cavalcade* is the best British film that has ever been made, and it was made in America."

The film played a three-week run at London's Tivoli Theatre, where it was viewed by 100,000 people. In the words of the *New York Times* (April 9, 1933), it had "given the British nation the finest 'boost' it has ever had on screen."

Cavalcade also brought Frank Lloyd his second Academy Award for Best Directing — it also won for Best Art Direction (William S. Darling) and, of course, Best Picture — and gave rise to a legendary Hollywood story. Frank Capra was positive that he would win the award (yet to be named "Oscar") for his direction of *Lady for a Day*, and at the ceremony on March 16, 1934, when master of ceremonies Will Rogers announced, "Come and get it, Frank," Capra headed for the podium only to realize too late, and with much embarrassment and humiliation, that it was Frank Lloyd who was being called. It is a story much repeated by Frank Capra, but, like so much of Hollywood history, untrue. In reality, Capra was called to the podium, along with George Cukor, after Lloyd had been given his Academy Award, in recognition of their coming in second and third in the balloting.[12] In 1935, Capra was to replace Lloyd as president of the Academy of Motion Picture Arts and Sciences.

Cavalcade was resurrected on two occasions for television. The Titanic scene was played by John Forsyth and Maria Riva (the daughter of Marlene Dietrich) as a sketch on *Ed Sullivan's Talk of the Town* on CBS on February 22, 1953. CBS also presented a forty-four minute version of the play on October 5, 1955, as part of the series, "The 20th Century-Fox Hour." Michael Wilding and Merle Oberon were the stars, and the production made ample use of the footage from the Frank Lloyd version. Also known as *Heart of a Woman*, the program was screened in British theatres in 1956.

In April 1933, Lloyd's agent, Edward Small, announced that the director would be leaving shortly for England to produce and direct an "epic" film there. It was not to be. Instead, Frank Lloyd began work, a month later, on a film which he generally described as his favorite, *Berkeley Square*.

With *Cavalcade* and to a certain extent with *East Lynne*, Frank Lloyd plays upon the American obsession with the British and British history, this country's curious preoccupation with all things English. And never more so than with *Berkeley Square*, in which a modern American inherits a London mansion and becomes, literally, part of its history.

The original source for *Berkeley Square* is Henry James 1917 unfinished novel, *The Sense of the Past*, but it is more accurately based on the play of the same name by John L. Balderston. *Berkeley Square* is the first film based on a work by Henry James.[13] He gets no screen credit, whereas Balderston is billed not only as the creator of the original but also co-screenwriter with Sonya Levien. Leslie Howard had co-produced, directed and starred in the original March 1929 production of the play in London, and also starred in the November 1929 Broadway production. He was brought to Hollywood to recreate his original role of Peter Standish, along with Valerie Taylor (Kate Pettigrew) and Irene Browne (Lady Ann Pettigrew).

One of the greatest of romantic screen melodramas (and a difficult one to view), *Berkeley Square* is also an unusual piece of science fiction, influential in the writings of H.P. Lovecraft, who saw the film three times, and obviously the source for Richard Matheson's *Bid Time Return*, filmed as *Somewhere in Time* in 1980.[14]

The storyline of *Berkeley Square* concerns an American, Peter Standish,[15] in 1930, who inherits a house in London's Berkeley Square. He is transported back in time to 1784 to become a wealthy American, Peter Standish, who has come to England, just after the War of Independence, to marry Kate Pettigrew. Instead, he falls in love with her sister, Helen. As the story unfolds, Standish reveals more than he should about what is to happen in the future, uses American slang terms of the 20th Century, and complains about hygiene — the English are horrified and amused that he insists on bathing on a daily basis. First, the painter Joshua Reynolds realizes that there is something supernatural about Peter Standish, and then members of the Pettigrew family, along with the Duchess of Devonshire, realize the same.

The film begins in 1784, moves forward to 1930, back to 1784, and concludes in 1930. At the end of the final period sequence, Helen (beautifully played by Heather Angel) tells Peter, "We'll be together, Peter, not in my time, nor in yours, but in *God's*." Those same words, spoken by Helen, are heard on the soundtrack as Peter in the present contemplates a lonely life in the Berkeley Square home. As well as those words, linking the past and the present is an Egyptian cross or *crux ansata*, symbolizing eternal life. Throughout, there is the concept, defined by Peter Standish that "Time, real time, is nothing but an idea in the mind of God."

Leslie Howard as Peter Standish in Berkeley Square.

There are some who have suggested that a director with a more romantic reputation, such as Frank Borzage, might have been more suited to handle the material, but the truth is that Lloyd's approach cannot be bettered. He links the two nations of Britain and the United States with appropriate patriotic airs, and throughout the use of music is subtle where necessary and lush when needed. Lloyd knows where to place the camera, where intimacy is required and where a more wider viewpoint is appropriate. He probably didn't need to direct Leslie Howard, whose performance is that of a neurotic hero, at first bemused and then forced tragically to face the reality of his character's situation: that he cannot change history, no matter how minor that history may be in the course of world events. The Peter Standish of the past married Kate, but he is in love with Helen. He must confess that this is the beginning: "this new age of speed and invention, which we shall never live to see." As the characters become horrified at the devilish knowledge of Peter Standish, so does he become disgusted with their ways and their bigotry.

Despite his obvious "Englishness," Leslie Howard plays the part as a true American. Early in the film, he is asked to drink a toast to the King. He does not join in, but instead drinks to the President of the United States and to "your King." It is very much Howard's film. He had been in American films since 1930, and his role goes a long way towards consolidating his success and fame in the United States. For his work here, Howard was nominated for an Academy Award for Best Actor.

The Production Code Administration removed a numbers of references to God from the script — "God knows," "Thank God," etc. — but not only left the story alone, but also praised it highly. Staff member James Wingate wrote to Will H. Hays, "It is an exquisite picture, beautifully acted and directed, and one which all lovers of clean pictures should get behind a hundred percent. If this picture proves a boxoffice flop, it will be a definite loss to the industry."[16]

Despite the obvious suggestion of "class" and "sophistication" here, audience reaction was most positive. There were two previews. The second, held at a Long Beach, California theatre, was attended by an "audience made up of sailors, shop girls, vacationists and just people," reported *Motion Picture Herald* (July 22, 1933). The trade paper continued that the response was as enthusiastic as that from the first screening, "where smart people predominate."

When *Berkeley Square* opened at New York's Gaiety Theatre, Mordaunt Hall in the *New York Times* (September 14, 1933) wrote that "nothing quite like it has emerged from Hollywood. It is an example of delicacy and restraint, a picture filled with gentle humor and appealing pathos. It is in a class by itself, which is not surprising, for Mr. Balderston had a hand in transforming the play into screen form and Frank Lloyd, who directed the memorable *Cavalcade*, officiated in the same capacity for this production…Mr. Lloyd has not missed an opportunity to do justice to camera possibilities."

Berkeley Square was remade by 20th Century-Fox in 1951, under the direction of Roy Baker, and starring Tyrone Power and Ann Blyth, as *I'll Never Forget You*; titled *The House on the Square* in the United Kingdom. 20th Century-Fox had planned a new version in 1945, for which Joseph L. Mankiewicz wrote an extant script.[17] There were television versions in 1949, 1951 and 1959, with the 1951 production starring Richard Greene and Grace Kelly. Unfortunately, while the studio was concentrating on remakes and productions in another medium, it was paying scant regard to the preservation of the original, and today the negative is long vanished — just as is the director's reputation.

1. Noel Coward, Present Indicative, Garden City, New York: Doubleday, Doran, 1937.

2. Quoted in Barry Day, Coward on Film: The Cinema of Noel Coward, pp. 24-25.

3. Jason S. Joy to the Fox studio executive Lamar Trotti, July 13, 1932. Production Code Administration file on Cavalcade, Margaret Herrick Library, Academy of Motion Picture Arts and Sciences.

4. Memorandum, May 17, 1932, ibid.

5. Winfield Sheehan to Frank Lloyd, July 1, 1932, ibid.

6. Quoted in Barry Day, Coward on Film: The Cinema of Noel Coward, p.26.

7. Quoted in Sheridan Morley, A Talent to Amuse: A Biography of Noel Coward, London: Heinemann, 1969, p. 172.

8. The version of Cavalcade that survives for viewing today is a British release print. However, it seems unlikely that there was any difference between the British and American versions.

9. With the Tide, p. 4.

10. Will Hays to James Wingate, January 6, 1933, Production Code Administration file on Cavalcade, Margaret Herrick Library, Academy of Motion Picture Arts and Sciences.

11. With the Tide, pp. 3-4.

12. Joseph McBride, Frank Capra: The Catastrophe of Success, New York: Simon & Schuster, 1992, p. 310.

13. American-born Henry James became a British citizen in 1915 in an effort to persuade Americans to support his adopted country in World War One

14. Howard Phillips Lovecraft, Selected Letters IV: 1932-1934, Sauk City, Wi.: Arkham House, 1976, pp. 362-371. I am indebted for this information to Craig Frischkorn, "Frank Lloyd's Berkeley Square (1933): Re-adapting Henry James's The Sense of the Past."

15. In the Henry James novel, the character is named Ralph Pendrel.

16. James Wingate to Will H. Hays, June 19, 1933, Production Code Administration file, Margaret Herrick Library, Academy of Motion Picture Arts and Sciences.

17. 20th Century-Fox production chief Darryl F. Zanuck dismissed the Lloyd version as "a colossal failure…The picture almost put the old Fox Company out of business," in an April 19, 1945 memorandum to Mankiewicz. The two men had a number of ideas as to who might star in their version including Tyrone Power, Henry Fonda, Gregory Peck, Jennifer Jones, Maureen O'Hara, and Jeanne Crain. Ultimately, Mankiewizc proposed Tyrone Power or Laurence Olivier, with Vivien Leigh as Helen and Maureen O'Hara as Kate. Of course, nothing came of the project. All information comes from the Joseph L. Mankiewicz Collection in the Margaret Herrick Library of the Academy of Motion Picture Arts and Sciences.

CHAPTER SIX

Mutiny on the Bounty

"For the period 1930-1940 Frank Lloyd remains one of the masters of adventure, one of those who introduced into the epic the story of time past, the exoticism, that undefinable soft and trembling feeling that is the attribute of American cinema," wrote the French critic Henri Agel. "Such is the common merit of *Cavalcade*, featuring the sober and aristocratic Clive Brook; of *Mutiny on the Bounty*, the cast of which remains one of the most dazzling in the history of the seventh art."[1]

Mutiny on the Bounty does boast a star-studded cast, a list of players that, in all probability, could only have been put together by MGM. Leading the group are Clark Gable, Charles Laughton and Franchot Tone, followed by some of the leading character men of the day, Hebert Mundin, Eddie Quillan, Dudley Digges, Donald Crisp, Henry Stephenson, and Lionel Belmore. Because of the nature of the story, there are few women, except for Spring Byington as Franchot Tone's mother and studio discovery Movita as Clark Gable's love interest, Tehani, on the island of Tahiti. At one point, Myrna Loy was announced for this role, but, happily, a change was made, just as equally fortuitously Wallace Beery and Robert Montgomery were replaced by Charles Laughton and Clark Gable. The latter was far from happy with the casting, angry at the costume he was forced to wear and the necessity to shave off his trademark moustache.

Frank Lloyd's production is based on two novels by Charles Nordhoff and James Norman Hall, *Mutiny on the Bounty* (1932) and *Men against the Sea* (1934), the first and second volumes in "The Bounty Trilogy." The April 28, 1789 mutiny on board his majesty's ship, the *Bounty*, had fascinated readers since the first book on the subject appeared in 1831, and there was little question that it would, to an equal extent, entertain moviegoers. The romantic vision of what took place, along with its aftermath, had long eclipsed any truth regarding the incident, in which undoubtedly Captain Bligh was far less villainous and Christian Fletcher less the dashing and heroic figure.[2]

When the first Nordhoff and Hall novel appeared, Lloyd paid the authors $20,000.00 for the movie rights, after earlier acquiring an option to the rights in partnership with his agent, Edward Small. When the second volume appeared, Lloyd paid them another $20,000.00, and for the screen rights to the third and final book in the trilogy, he upped the offer to $22,000.00. It was rejected, and nor was he able to purchase the rights to another Nordhoff and Hall novel, *The Hurricane*, which Samuel Goldwyn acquired for $60,000.00. The producer approached Lloyd to direct the screen adaptation, but the director refused, recommending Howard Hawks in his place. The film was eventually made in 1937 with John Ford directing.

Some modern sources erroneously suggest that Lloyd purchased the story in order that he might not only direct but also play the role of Captain Bligh. Apparently, in that both men had bushy eyebrows, Lloyd was a natural for the part. It is not known if the director made such a request to Metro-Goldwyn-Mayer, when he sold the studio the rights, but it seems very unlikely. Lloyd had initially intended to produce the film for release by Fox. It is not difficult to understand how much the Bounty mutiny could have appealed to Lloyd. Here is a story that combines two elements with which he always had such a close affinity: the sea and British history. Even if he had not been in a strong negotiating position as owner of the screen rights, there was not another director in Hollywood at this time remotely qualified to handle such a story, such a theme, such a historical spectacle.

In order to avoid any potential competition, MGM acquired the rights to a 1933 Australian film on the mutiny, *In the Wake of the Bounty*, written, produced and directed by Charles Chauvel, and starring a young actor named Errol Flynn as Fletcher Christian. Both the film and Flynn's performance are mediocre. It is coincidental that a few years later, the actor was to star in a 1940 "remake" of *The Sea Hawk*, for which the studio, Warner Bros, completely jettisoned the original story.

There was no question but that Frank Lloyd would be the film's director, but Irving Thalberg assumed the role of production while allowing Lloyd to participate in the capacity of what was then called associate producer (a far more important and very different position to that implied by the credit today). The associate producer position allowed Lloyd the opportunity to involve himself heavily in the editing process, which he did by providing cutting suggestions to Albert Lewin and Margaret Booth.[3]

In fact, MGM was already familiar with the storyline, having read the first volume in galley form, but expressing no major interest in it. Talbot Jennings was assigned the task of writing the screenplay, which he later shared with Jules Furthman and Carey Wilson. Jennings' original script had the film opening in Portsmouth Harbor in 1934, with a shot of *H.M.S. Hood*. The scene cuts to the warrant officers' mess with the captain's speaking, suggesting that the world should know of the suffering of the men on the *Bounty*.[4] The scene then dissolves to 1787. The opening was rejected a couple of months later, in August 1934, as taking away from the original story.

As always with Frank Lloyd, pre-production included an extensive period of research. The *New York Times* (November 3, 1935) reported,

"In the first place, fourteen months of diligent research work, conducted by a corps of delvers into old books and records, provided the film company with an accurate record of everything from the length of the Bounty foresail to the width of Captain Bligh's shoes. Every possible bit of documentation relating to the Bounty's last trip was consulted, and every bit of sea and soil across which the band of mutineers traveled was scaled and studied by the executives working on the story."

Background footage was shot in the South Seas as early as February 1935, but the film was found to have been underexposed, and the trip had to be repeated. Two replicas of *H.M.S. Bounty* were built, one was sailed to Tahiti and the second was moored at Santa Catalina Island, off the coast of California. Portsmouth Harbor was recreated here, as well as a number of Polynesian villages. Filming also took place on Pitcairn Island and on San Miguel Island, off the coast of Santa Barbara. In all, *Mutiny on the Bounty* was in production from May through September 1935.

While expressing "great interest and admiration" for the original script, Joseph Breen of the Production Code Administration wrote to MGM's Louis B. Mayer that there were problems with the amount of brutality, the bawdy atmosphere on board the *Bounty* and, most crucially, the clothing, or lack of it, of the Tahitian men and women. "You will realize that scenes showing the nude breasts of women, even native women, are not only in violation of the Production Code, but are invariably cut by all censor boards," he wrote.[5]

Further versions of the script were submitted to Breen between December 1934 and February 1935, and most requested eliminations made. The main concern remained scenes between Christian and Byam and the two native girls. "We presume that your camera angles and distances, as well as the use of loin cloths and flowers, will meet the requirements of the Code," wrote Breen, also pointing out that "no backward and forward motion of the hips or rolling of the abdomen" could be permitted in the native dance and that there could be no "horizontal kissing" between Christian and Maimiti.[6] As late as October 1935, the Production Code Administration was still unwilling to issue a certificate because of "several scenes in which Clark Gable and a native girl are seen lying on the ground embracing. As you know, this horizontal lovemaking has always proved questionable on account of the sex connotations which such scenes inevitably bring to mind."[7]

The film opens in December 1787 in Portsmouth, following an introductory title explaining what the story is about and also exalting British sea power. Clark Gable is introduced as Fletcher Christian, leading a press gang and capturing six men in a pub. These unwilling volunteers will serve as crewmen on the Bounty which is due to sail to Tahiti to pick up breadfruit trees and bring them to the West Indies, as a cheap source of food for slaves. The manner in which the ordinary seamen are pressed into service is compared to the manner in which Franchot Tone as Roger Byam accepts his appointment as a midshipman on the Bounty, with his duties including the research for a Tahitian dictionary. His mother's comment that "a taut hand at sea is better than a slack one" is one that does not take into account the cruelty of the Bounty's captain, William Bligh.

His ordering the bosun to flog a dead man while the ship is still at anchor in Portsmouth harbor emphasizes the violence of Captain Bligh aboard the Bounty. The growing animosity between Fletcher Christian and Captain Bligh is apparent at the start of the Bounty's journey, but it is very obvious that these two men have something very much in common — they both love the ship and they love the sea. Nevertheless, Fletcher Christian (and the audience) are horrified by a series of vignettes illustrating Bligh's cruel and inhuman punishments, including keelhauling and the tying of a sailor to a gun barrel where he is flogged. Even Byam is not above suffering such punishment as he is forced to stand on top of the masthead during a storm.

The mood changes with the Bounty's arrival in Tahiti. The pace slows and a romantic quality emerges. Captain Bligh seems momentarily to calm down before reminding his crew that they are there to labor not to enjoy themselves with the native women. In fact, the film is at its weakest at this point as the encounters between sailor and Tahitians seem artificial and very much on a par with the typical Hollywood vision of the South Seas. "What a contrast," remarks Fletcher Christian of life on the island to life on the ship. And what a contrast there is to the believable melodrama of the first half of the film compared to Hollywood's concept of an idyllic society and romance. "This island isn't real," say the Franchot

Tone character. And it is as unreal as Clark Gable's donning of a carefully tailored and laundered loincloth, with the emphasis on his pectoral and upper arm muscles. He seems a would-be Johnny Weissmuller auditioning for the role of Tarzan.

John Mosher, writing in *The New Yorker* (November 16, 1935) voiced a similar opnion: "Frank Lloyd has handled the whole shipload well, except

An obviously posed shot of Clark Gable and Movita in Mutiny on the Bounty.

in Tahiti. Tahiti always gets Hollywood a little unnerved, and, as the picture is long, those Tahiti romances, Tahiti *leis* and so on, might have been cut quite a bit. You've seen that kind of thing a lot. You haven't seen anything quite as good as the rest of the film." Not all critics would agree. In describing the scenes on Tahiti, French critic Henri Agel evokes Rousseau and Chateaubriand. "Actually it is in no way literary," he continues,

Clark Gable as Fletcher Christian orders Charles Laughton as Captain Bligh off the Bounty in Mutiny on the Bounty.

"it is halfway between an inebriated sensation, an anticipated regret, and an indefinably prolonged dream. This accord between a moment of the story and a *mise en scene* so physically true is one of the great secrets of American films."[8]

So unacceptable are the Tahitian scenes that it seems not before time when Fletcher Christian seizes control of the Bounty, a mutiny that takes place following the ship's aged physician's unnecessary death after he is forced to witness the flogging of four seaman who have attempted to desert. The takeover of the ship is, again, Frank Lloyd at his best, shooting as if this was a silent film, with the minimum of non-natural sound. There is just a quiet, and ominous, intensity to the fury of the mutineers' actions. From this point onwards, the film moves to its inevitable conclusion. Captain Bligh and his few supporters are cast adrift in an open boat.

Here is the purist of melodramatic scenes, not just the "hanging from the highest yardarm in the British fleet" lines, but also Bligh's prayer to God in the small boat. There is not a word slurred or imprecise. It is vocalized hatred and anguish — hatred toward the mutineers and anguish at losing the *Bounty*. This is a sequence matched only by Franchot Tone's impassioned speech at his court martial.

Fletcher Christian turns the ship around, returning to Tahiti, where he picks up the native woman with whom he has fallen in love, along with other native women. In Tahiti, Christian leaves Byam, together with other sailors who did not wish to participate in the mutiny. He then sails on to Pitcairn Island, where he burns the Bounty for fear that it may be spotted by a passing British frigate. In the meantime, Byam and the others are picked up by a British ship, taken to England, and at the insistence of Bligh, tried at a court martial, sentenced to death, but subsequently pardoned by the King. Byam begins a new naval career on board Lord Nelson's flagship, about to participate in the battle of Trafalgar, and the film concludes with what would seem almost an obligatory playing of "Rule Britannia."

Filming was not without incident. An assistant cameraman, Glenn Strong, was killed and a number of technicians injured when a barge being used for second unit shooting capsized off San Miguel Island on July 25, 1935.

Lloyd was also forced to contend with two leading men who actively hated each other. In their scenes together, Charles Laughton refused to look at Clark Gable, who complained to the director. Only producer Irving Thalberg's arrival diffused the situation. However, no sooner did Thalberg depart than both actors turned on Lloyd, accusing him of failing to provide them with sufficient direction. Again, Thalberg was called in.

The attack by the actors on the director is obviously unjustified. As Lloyd explained a year later,

"I usually make very big, very important and exceptionally expensive productions…and I can't afford to take any chances. It isn't so much the question of an actor's ability, because that's taken for granted if we even consider him, but of his rating with the public. If we put box-office names into a picture, we automatically assure ourselves a good box-office receipt. Naturally, once I've settled the worth of a player from that standpoint, I try to get the best work out of him. On the other hand I don't cast people just because their names are good; I have to consider the personal aura they've built around themselves."[9]

According to *The Hollywood Reporter* (August 2, 1935), *Mutiny on the Bounty* was the most expensive MGM production up to this time, costing between $1,800,000.00 and $2,000,000.00. In all, at least 131 million feet of film was shot, at least 1,000 feet of which was used for the short subject *Pitcairn's Island Today*, released by MGM in September 1935 as obvious pre-publicity for *Mutiny on the Bounty*.

Captain Bligh's descendants were not overly happy with the production. Their spokesman, a New York writer and architect named Frederick Bligh Bond, noted that "Capt. Bligh contributed a great deal of scientific and geographic information of present-day value to mariners, and he deserved to be remembered for that as well as the fact that he was a kind and loving husband and father, and a faithful friend…You must remember that Capt. Bligh was a self-made man who won his position from the ranks whereas the mutineers were led by disgruntled aristocrats."[10]

Those voices defending the reputation of Captain Bligh were scarcely heard above the praise for the film and the man portraying the infamous sea captain. *The Hollywood Reporter* (October 28, 1935) assigned its review to the front page, describing the film as one of the greatest of all time: "Twelve years ago Frank Lloyd compelled world-wide attention with his direction of *The Sea Hawk*, accounted at the time a milestone in motion picture progress, now with his masterful direction of this great epic drama of the sea, the world has a chance to see what amazing progress has been made in the art of the screen and to witness the maturing of a great talent."

Other trade papers were equally effusive, with *Motion Picture Herald* (November 9, 1935) writing, "*Mutiny on the Bounty* is melodrama, the ripping, tearful power of which leaves one breathless." While *Variety* (November 13, 1935) complained of the running time of 131 minutes being too long for most exhibitors, it had to admit that "As a production of the type that used to be known as a 'spectacle,' and as an example of superb screen authorship and as an exhibition of compelling histrionics, this one is Hollywood at its very best. The story certainly could not be presented as powerfully through any other medium."

When *Mutiny on the Bounty* opened in New York at the Capitol Theatre on November 8, 1935, the critics there were equally enthusiastic. "The motion picture spectacle as it should be conceived," wrote the *Herald-Tribune*; "To see it once is to remember it always," commented the *American*; "little short of a masterpiece," was the opinion of the *Post*; "Frank Lloyd keeps events leading to ever mounting degree of excitement until they reach smashing climax," noted the *News*.[11] While reserving principal praise for Charles Laughton, describing his performance as "a fascinating and almost unbearable portrait of a sadist who took rapturous delight in watching men in pain," Andre Sennwald in the *New York Times*

(November 9, 1935) wrote that the story was "magnificently transferred to the screen," containing "the stuff of half a dozen adventure pictures. It is superlatively thrilling."

It was, naturally, Laughton who received the most generous portions of praise. Typical is Mark Van Doren in *The Nation* (January 1, 1936):

"Charles Laughton, whose performance as Captain Bligh in *Mutiny on the Bounty*, fixes him in my mind at any rate as by far the best of living actors. I had thought him that before, but the current picture leaves no room for doubt. Frank Lloyd's direction has amplitude and clarity, and the film has many other merits besides the chief one — its making use of such an artist. It is Mr. Laughton, however, whom we watch; and I cannot believe that this is to be accounted for on any other theory than that he has resources beyond the power of even the most brilliant direction to conceive. No man could be told to do what he does. He would have to know how — to know, for instance, how to *be* Captain Bligh, and how to be him in such fullness that no inconsistency appeared between the tyrant of the Bounty and the hero of the open boat on that impossible voyage to Timor."

The British critics were equally impressed when *Mutiny on the Bounty* opened there in January 1936, noting that it was in reality a patriotic British picture. *The Sunday Times* compared it to the Russian *Potemkin*. The London *Evening News*, with lovely British understatement, called it "a grand bit of movie-making." In *The Observer*, C.A. Lejeune wrote, "We are justified in a fairly sentimental gesture of gratitude to America...Charles Laughton's Captain Bligh is a stubbornly regimented study of a man who had no grandeur except in pettiness. Clark Gable's Fletcher Christian gives him the right to be called an actor at last, and not a film star. Franchot Tone had many of the most successful moments, and the best lines of Talbot Jennings' lovely English dialogue tell to his share."[12]

Elsewhere in the world, there was similar enthusiasm. Only in Japan was it banned outright, and, in Spain, it was cut so severely by the censors that it was unreleasable. There was, of course, some opposition to the film's British outlook. In Italy and Ireland, shots of the Union Jack were eliminated as were positive references to England. Also in Ireland, the performance of "Rule Britannia" was deleted.

Mutiny on the Bounty received eight Academy Awards nominations — Best Picture, Best Actor (Clark Gable, Franchot Tone and Charles Laughton), Best Director, Best Screenplay (Talbot Jennings, Jules Furthman and Carey Wilson), Best Film Editing (Margaret Booth), and Best Score (Herbert Stothart) — but won only in the Best Picture category.

Frank Lloyd's last seafaring melodrama (if one ignores, as one should, *This Woman Is Mine*) has a far more modern and down-to-earth quality to it, but there is little question that *Rulers of the Sea* was very close to its director's heart. It is basically the story of a sail-and-steam vessel, setting out from Greenock, on the River Clyde, in Scotland for New York on March 28, 1838. Just as *Mutiny on the Bounty* is the director's tribute to the Royal Navy, *Rulers of the Sea* is his salute to the Merchant Marine. As the film's foreword discloses,

"*Rulers of the Sea* is respectfully dedicated to the merchant marine of the world, whose high standards of speed and safety were made possible through the earnest struggles and stirring achievements of those early pioneers with whom this fictional story, inspired by facts, is concerned."

The film reunites Lloyd with Talbot Jennings, who had co-written the screenplay for *Mutiny on the Bounty*, and here developed the story and screenplay along with Frank Cavett and Richard Collins. Waldo Twitchell, who had been responsible for the same task on *If I Were King* and *Wells Fargo*, undertook research and Dutch-born composer Richard Hageman, who had made his screen debut with the score for *If I Were King*, was signed to write the score for *Rulers of the Sea*.

Douglas Fairbanks, Jr. is the leading man, playing a young sailing mate, converted to the notion of steam and pioneering its use in transatlantic navigation. He is not particularly believable in the role; he gives the impression that he is more suited to an admiral's uniform than that of a first mate. British actress Margaret Lockwood provides the romantic interest, and Scottish character actor Will Fyffe adds nominal humor as a visionary mechanic based in Greenock. This was Fyffe's only American screen appearance. British audiences best knew him for his music hall appearances, singing "I Belong to Glasgow," a sentiment that must have been most appealing to the film's Glasgow-born director. Fyffe was singled out for special praise by Robert W. Dana in the *New York Herald Tribune* (November 9, 1939), with his comment, "It is a stirring screen epic that must fight all the way from being out-classed in brilliance by the acting of Will Fyffe, who, in his first American picture, makes the role of a disillusioned, oft-disappointed machine-shop worker one of the most human and moving the screen has offered this year."

As they do in *Rulers of the Sea*, Lockwood and Fyffe had previously played daughter and father in the 1938 British film, *Owd Bob*, released in the U.S. as *To the Victor*. However, the real stars of the film were the two ships battling each other across the Atlantic. As John Mosher wrote in *The New Yorker* (November 11, 1939), the film was "told with simple schoolroom care," and "So handsome are the sea and ship scenes that the actors can't assert themselves to any special degree."

Dog Star is the paddle steamer making history as the first vessel to cross the Atlantic using steam power, and the *Falcon*, a full-rigged sailing ship of the packet type with skysails as high as 170 feet above the water line is its losing competitor. These two ships were recreated from two extant

Will Fyffe and Douglas Fairbanks, Jr. in Rulers of the Sea.

vessels; the *Golden State* from the Atlantic fisheries service became the *Dog Star*, while the *Metha Nelson* was rebuilt as the *Falcon*. The rebuilding took place over a three-month period in a dry dock at Los Angeles Harbor, under the direction of John Goodman, the unit art director, and marine expert James Havens. It was Havens who supervised the actual use of the ships at sea off Santa Catalina, San Miguel and San Clemente Islands, just as he had been responsible for the ships in *Mutiny on the Bounty*.

Aside from the ships, Lloyd also build an exact replica of the *Dog Star*'s engine room, along with two Greenock machine shops, and recreated the waterfronts of London and Greenock at the Los Angeles Harbor. The film illustrates the sort of attention to detail that Lloyd so delighted in but which probably had little resonance with the audience. Lloyd's overconcentration on detail obviously bothered some critics. When *Rulers of the Sea* opened in New York at the Paramount Theatre, Frank S. Nugent in the *New York Times* (November 9, 1939) described it as a "handsomely produced film which possesses everything but the spark that kindles interest into enthusiasm — not dramatic at all." (The film had received its world premiere at the Carthay Circle Theatre in Los Angeles on September 12, 1939.)

Rulers of the Sea is also the closest that Frank Lloyd was to come on screen to his native Scotland. He might have been Scottish, but his British films are very rooted in England and the English way of life, the English sense of honor. Only here does he have the opportunity, obviously on a far lesser scale than *Cavalcade*, to pay tribute to a very important part of Scottish heritage, the shipbuilding industry on the Clyde.

In May 1940, Lloyd announced plans for a sequel to *Mutiny on the Bounty*, to be released by Universal. The film would again star Charles Laughton as Captain Bligh, and deal with his career as governor of the Australian penal colony. Because the actor could not return to the United States for tax reasons, Lloyd planned to shoot Laughton's scenes in England. Spencer Tracy was to be cast opposite Laughton, and the film had at least three tentative titles: *Capt. Bligh*, *Capt. Bligh in Australia* and *Capt. Bligh Returns*. Nothing came of the project. The *Mutiny on the Bounty* saga continued in 1962 with a disastrous remake by director Lewis Milestone (who took over the assignment from British director Carol Reed), which boasted a stunning visual quality and good supporting performances by Trevor Howard, Richard Harris and Hugh Griffith, but a mediocre characterization of Fletcher Christian by Marlon Brando. Equally disappointing was a 1984 remake by Australian director Roger Donaldson, titled simply *The Bounty*, which featured Mel Gibson, Anthony Hopkins and Laurence Olivier and attempted, sadly without much success, to reconsider Fletcher Christian and Captain Bligh in less than the strong black-and-white characterizations adopted by Frank Lloyd.

---

1. Henri Agel, Romance Américaine, Paris: Editions du Cerf, 1963, p. 46. Prior to Mutiny on the Bounty, Lloyd directed Servant's Entrance for Fox. Released in September 1934, the film reunited Janet Gaynor and Lew Ayres who had worked so well together in State Fair. It is primarily of interest for a dream sequence animated by the Walt Disney Studios.

2. The 1831 volume, written by Sir John Barrow, is titled The Eventful History of the Mutiny and Piratical Seizure of H.M.S. Bounty. The next book on the subject, and even more popular, is Lady Diana Belcher's The Mutineers of the Bounty and Their Descendants, published in 1831. The most recent, and most accurate account, is Caroline Alexander's The Bounty: The True Story of the Mutiny on the Bounty, New York: Viking, 2003.

3. Memorandum dated June 18, 1935, Metro-Goldwyn-Mayer Screenplay Collection, Cinema Library, University of Southern California.

4. Script dated June 27, 1934, Metro-Goldwyn-Mayer Screenplay Collection, Cinema Library, University of Southern California.

5. Letter dated December 26, 1934, Production Code Administration file, Margaret Herrick Library of the Academy of Motion Picture Arts and Sciences.

6. Letter dated February 27, 1935.

7. Letter dated October 15, 1935.

8. Henri Agel, Romance Américaine, Paris: Editions du Cerf, 1963, p. 47.

9. Quoted in Howard Sharpe, "The Star Creators of Hollywood: Frank Lloyd," p. 102.

10. Quoted in Corbin Patrick, "Capt. Bligh of 'Bounty' No Inhuman Sadist, New York Descendant Says," Indianapolis Star, November 16, 1935.

11. Reviews excerpted in The Hollywood Reporter, November 11, 1935.

12. Reviews excerpted in The Hollywood Reporter, January 18, 1936.

Frank Lloyd, third from left, directs Under Two Flags. *Assistant director Ad Schaumer is to his right, script girl Lee Frederick sits below them, and Cliff Maupin is at the still camera.*

CHAPTER SEVEN

The Paramount Features

After completion of *Mutiny on the Bounty*, Frank Lloyd returned to 20th Century-Fox for one last film, *Under Two Flags*, prior to moving on to Paramount, where he had last worked in the 1920s. Not only was it Lloyd's last production for the company but it was also star Ronald Colman's last contractual film for the studio. Ronald Colman was to star for Lloyd not only in *Under Two Flags*, but also in *If I Were King*, the director's penultimate film for Paramount. Both are French-themed, and very much melodramas, but they are very different in setting, time and subject. The first is set in a Southern Algerian Foreign Legion outpost in the late 19th Century, and the second in Paris of the 1460s.

Shot in part on location in the Arizona desert, the sixth screen version of the Ouida novel, *Under Two Flags*, provides its star with the somewhat difficult role of Sergeant Victor, loved by two women and fighting in the Legion to compensate somehow for a crime committed by his brother but for which he has taken responsibility. It is very much in the classic melodramatic mode of *Beau Geste* — but, ultimately, not as good or as satisfying.

The battle scenes in *Under Two Flags* were the work of associate director Otto Brower, and, in all probability, Frank Lloyd did not spend much time on location. He was busy at the studio with the more intimate scenes, which most critics agreed were not entirely convincing. Unfortunately, the swift and well-engineered battle scenes emphasized the slow pacing of the footage shot at the studio. Lloyd's work was not helped by the temperamental behavior of the film's initial female star, Simone Simon, in what was to be the French actress's first production for the studio after several months of idleness. As reported in the *New York Times* (February 2, 1936), on the set, whenever anything unpleasant occurred, Simon would place a thermometer in her mouth and claim a temperature of 105. After two weeks of shooting, and concerned how the actress would behave in the heat of a desert location, Lloyd demanded the studio replace Simon, which it did with the much higher-priced Claudette Colbert.

Under Two Flags was produced between December 1935 and March 1936. When Lloyd had finished with the film, he was well satisfied. Studio

Left to right: Herbert Mundin, Ronald Colman, Nigel Bruce, and Claudette Colbert in Under Two Flags.

head Darryl F. Zanuck was not, and arbitrarily cut the film along with another recently completed production, John Ford's *Prisoner of Shark Island*. Both Lloyd and Ford were incensed and announced that they would never again work at 20th Century-Fox. Ford did eventually return, but Lloyd stayed true to his vow. Ford and Lloyd were drinking buddies, as close as two directors could be, despite, as one writer pointed out, they were "at the furthest odds, so far as their particular approaches and attitudes are concerned."[1]

The cutting of his films without his oversight was a matter of which Frank Lloyd had long expressed outrage. As early as 1920, he harangued local exhibitors who would cut down his productions to meet their screening schedules. "After the producer, director and film editor have labored over a photoplay with great care, it is no joy to hear that theatre managers in the smaller towns are using the shears to ruin their best efforts," he was quoted.²

As with all productions at his studio, Darryl F. Zanuck had kept close watch over the scripting process. Prior to the merger of his Twentieth Century Pictures with the Fox Film Corporation, the latter had acquired the rights to the story from Universal, which had a remake in the plan-

Directing a scene with Victor McLaglen and Jamiel Hassen in Under Two Flags. *Frank Lloyd stands beside the hat.*

ning stage. As early as August 1935, Zanuck decided that the production should not be updated but should play in the period in which it was originally written. An early draft script by W.P. Lipscomb was greeted with scorn by the production head,

"The plot is swell. The continuity is great. The dialog is awful. The heavy is nothing but a movie villain. There is not a genuine character in the piece...

"But if we take this continuity and write real human beings, simply understandable characters, into it, there is no question but we will have a picture more terrific than *Bengal Lancers*."³

The critics were divided as to the worth of the production. The attitude of many was summed up by John Mosher in *The New Yorker* (May

9, 1936), "Too much sand." "Costly, handsome and overlong," was the opinion of *Time* (May 11, 1936), while Robert Stebbins wrote in *New Theatre* (June 1936), "A waste of excellent cast, proficient photography, and your good hour and a half." In the *New York Herald Tribune* (May 1, 1936), Howard Barnes wrote,

"The striking pictorial beauty of *Under Two Flags* does not cloak a multitude of dramatic sins...Liberties have been taken with [Ouida's] preposterous and sentimental literary bow to the French Foreign Legion, but the narrative still creaks embarrassingly and the photoplay cries out for extensive cutting...It is probable that no amount of retouching would serve to invigorate the musty Ouida knickknack. The story is a confusion of melodramatic adventures and improbably love affairs that defy a plausible screen pattern."

Most criticism was directed at the original source material: "a worn-out formula," wrote the *Christian Science Monitor* (May 2, 1936), while *Rob Wagner's Script* described it as "grand old hokem drammer." Frank Lloyd fared better: "deft direction," opined Frank S. Nugent in the *New York Times* (May 1, 1936).

"My filming of *If I Were King* prompted many persons to ask me," wrote Frank Lloyd, "Why, they want to know, do I seemingly prefer to go back into history for my screen subjects?

"*If I Were King* is being made because of no preference of mine for period stories. It is being made because I sincerely believe it to be one of the great romances of all time. Its characters are vital. The incidents which give rise to their actions and reactions are born of exciting times. Their attitudes are believable and understandable.

"Francois Villon was a rascal: a rabble rousing mischief maker with a flair for poetry. But history and legend combined have him a completely charming rascal whose appeal has not been dimmed through almost five centuries.

"It must be remembered that the courtly romance of the Middle Ages or any other hand-kissing era is not frowned upon by modern womanhood. The more there is of sophistication, of feminine equality in the modern scheme of things, the more, I believe, will women hunger for romance."

If Ronald Colman is somewhat hard to accept as a dashing Legionnaire, he is equally difficult to endorse as poet and rogue Francois Villon, a characterization best brought to life by John Barrymore in 1927 in *The Beloved Rogue*. Colman is at his best playing Villon the poet rather than Villon, the likeable villain. Many would argue that the film, produced between May and July 1938, succeeds in large part thanks to its screenwriter Preston Sturges, who provides the star with dialogue he can sincerely deliver. At the same time, while it is true that Frank Lloyd may not have been totally at ease with Sturges' cynicism, it is the director who obtains the performance and delivery from Colman. He also manages to obtain some convincing swordplay from the aging actor (although, in all fairness, Colman is little older than Barrymore was when he played the

Ronald Colman as Francois Villon in If I Were King.

part). Preston Sturges and Frank Lloyd worked well together, with the former considering the director a tasteful and intelligent one.

Frank Lloyd purportedly told Preston Sturges that he should direct as well as write: "There's going to be a revolution soon in screen writing. We've been mixing screen technique with the technique of the stage, and it hasn't been wholly satisfactory. There should be a new kind of writing,

Frank Lloyd with his associate producer (and former screenwriter) Howard Estabrook on Maid of Salem.

adaptable only to the screen. Authors are being encouraged, and I think that authors/producers will arise."⁴

There were some critics who were in agreement with *Time* (October 3, 1938) that the film's "makers have found not one fresh point of view, have included every available cliché of sword-&-cloak romance, plus the cliché of modern fiction, social significance. Result: so wooden that even the clashing of swords suggests a xylophone." However, on the whole, the production was extremely well received. *Newsweek* (October 10, 1938) wrote that "Lloyd has given *If I Were King* a fine cast and handsome trapping; as director, he has kept acres of Gothic sets and an army of extras from swamping the fresh characterizations with which he streamlines an old-fashioned romance." "It is old-fashioned stuff, in which you can hear the plot creaking as well as the armor," noted Howard Barnes in the *New York Herald Tribune* (September 29, 1938), "but it is handsomely and engagingly set forth."

Frank Lloyd's first Paramount production, *Maid of Salem*, reunited him with his *Under Two Flags* leading lady, Claudette Colbert. Produced between August and November 1936, the film was shot at the studio, the

Fred MacMurray and Claudette Colbert in Maid of Salem.

Paramount Ranch, north of Los Angeles, and a location outside of Santa Cruz, standing in for old Salem Village of 1692. The Salem witchcraft trials are prominent in early American history, and yet, surprisingly, this is the first to deal with the subject in depth.

In part a study of mob psychology, *Maid of Salem* opens slowly as Lloyd sets the scene, showing the audience a Puritan village in all its quaint, and sometimes not so quaint, aspects. The storyline leads up to the prattle about witchcraft spoken by spiteful children, led by Bonita Granville, who did much the same amount of lying in *These Three*, Goldwyn's adaptation of Lillian Hellman's *The Children's Hour*. From the slow pacing of the early scenes, the film picks up speed, the direction taking on a briskness as the plot moves to its old-fashioned melodramatic conclusion, with Fred MacMurray galloping upon a horseback to save Claudette Colbert from the gallows. Perhaps one of the weakest elements in the film is the casting of MacMurray who always looks decidedly ill at ease in a period costume. However, as the critic in *Stage* (March 1937) commented, "Once the panic of witchcraft starts (and you know what Director Frank Lloyd did with panic in *Cavalcade* and *Mutiny*), you are carried along on a vicious crescendo of madness and terror."

The script, very carefully researched by Frank Lloyd and his writers, led by Bradley King, initially had the Claudette Colbert character being burned at the stake. It was Joseph Breen, head of the Production Code Administration, who pointed out that, despite legend, witches in Salem were hanged. It must have been something of an irritation for the accuracy-obsessed Frank Lloyd to have a mistake in the script pointed out to him by the head of Hollywood's self-censoring authority. *Maid of Salem* was, in all probability, the first of Lloyd's for which he had appointed a formal head of technical research. The appointee was Lance Baxter, who had previously undertaken research for the director on *Cavalcade* and *Under Two Flags*.[5]

The manner in which Lloyd approached *Maid of Salem* typifies his concern for the budget, where to cut and where to spend, regardless of what studio is paying the bill:

"*Maid of Salem* opened at $1,000,000, but after a week of thought we got it down to $900,000 without losing any quality at all…We saved on little things, not big ones. About this location here at Santa Cruz. We found out it would cost just a thousand dollars more to put up in a deluxe camp than in hotels, but I'd rather be near the set and we can always save that money some other way. Shoot ahead of schedule or something… Then just start in and make the picture."[6]

Where Lloyd would not penny pinch was in his concern for authenticity. *Maid of Salem* could have been shot on a soundstage, but it was not, because the moviegoing public would notice the artificiality. The equation was simple: if the product was artificial, the public would not be there, and with no audience there would be no money.

Certainly, the critics helped encourage attendance, with *Time* (March 8, 1937) describing the film as "a lurid page of colonial history" and John Mosher in *The New Yorker*, praising Lloyd for turning "out some really startling bits of Puritan lore." In her February 19, 1937 syndicated column, Louella Parsons wrote, "it has remained for Frank Lloyd to give us the most powerful indictment and most realistic story of those nerve racking days." (Only Louella could have described the Salem witch hunt as "nerve racking.") When the film *Maid of Salem* opened at the Paramount Theatre, the *New York Times* (March 4, 1937) hailed Lloyd as "the shrewd Scot who seems to have a flair for romanticizing matters of record for the screen without tampering too seriously with the record, [adding] an important film chapter to his growing volume of historical highlights."

Maid of Salem was followed by another piece of historical Americana, but this time far more sweeping in its scope and presentation. *Wells Fargo* is the story of the development of American transportation. As Louella Parsons described it in her December 31, 1937 syndicated gossip column, "a stirring cavalcade of early American transportation." The use of the word "cavalcade" is perhaps not coincidental in that there must have been some thought in the minds of both the director and the producer that this was an American response to *Cavalcade*, but in an earlier period of history and with war replaced by the pony express and the stagecoach. The original working title, *An Empire Is Born*, suggests that this is a new *Birth of a Nation*, set not against a background of the Civil War or the Boer War and World War One, as with *Cavalcade*, but rather the expansion and growth of the American West and its mode of transportation and communication. Unfortunately, *Wells Fargo* is a brave effort, but it is no *Cavalcade*.

When Lloyd joined Paramount, he had told a reporter that, "It's about time that we made a really 'great' American picture — one with a real national spirit…the sort of story I have in mind would be to this country what *Cavalcade* was to England."[7]

With a reported budget of $1,500,000, *Wells Fargo* was filmed in the summer of 1937 at various California locations, including the Napa Valley and Chico, and at the Paramount Ranch, where what was claimed to be the largest set ever made — of San Francisco's Portsmouth Square in the 1850s and 1860s — was constructed. The personal drama involves Wells Fargo messenger Ramsay MacKay, played by Joel McCrea, and his wife, Southerner Justine, played by McCrea's real wife Frances Dee, reunited here with Lloyd after her performance as the leading lady in *If I Were King*. Encompassing the human story are seven distinct episodes covering the period 1844-1870.

Howard Estabrook was Lloyd's associate producer on *Maid of Salem*, promoted to full-fledged producer for *Wells Fargo*. The two men proved a good, working combination, with both strong believers in research and willing to spend time carefully reviewing the script prior to shooting. Lloyd must also have been pleased to work with the man responsible for the 1935 screen adaptation of Charles Dickens' *David Copperfield*.

Writing in *Foremost Films of 1938*, critic Frank Vreeland commented, "*Wells Fargo* is a prime example of the adaptability of the screen to the chronicle play. Aside from a few notable examples like *Abraham Lincoln* and *Murder in the Cathedral* the stage has never been really successful with this form even at the hands of Shakespeare, especially in the modern theatre…The quick, shifting flexibility of the screen makes it a more suitable medium for such work than even the Elizabethan stage. The speed with which divergent locales can be interpolated and yet knit together offers the beholder an engrossing sense of variety. Such a panoramic scope gives great sweep to a historical subject like *Wells Fargo*. Yet though it covers

Joel McCrea in Wells Fargo.

a longer period than Drinkwater's play about the Great Emancipator it conveys less sense of sprawling development."[8]

Most critics raised an issue which is often raised with Frank Lloyd's productions. The research is superb and detailed, but often overwhelms the humanity of the story. Performances are often secondary to the production values. "The film is a little too long, and too many of its people are conscious of the history they are helping to make," complained Mark Van Doren in *The Nation* (January 15, 1938). "Its research is endless, its material fascinating," wrote Otis Ferguson in *The New Republic* (January 5, 1938), "But history is not enough, and so over everything we must have the false uninteresting life and love of Joel McCrea…It runs two hours, by the end of which time it is firmly settled as the towering bore of the season." In summation, as *Stage* (February 1938) put it, "The makings are epic, the finished product is not."

One critic who was not kind was NBC's Alistair Cooke who described *Wells Fargo* on a January 5, 1938 broadcast as "the longest teaser in the history of motion pictures — a ninety minute trailer to a film that was never made." Paramount threatened NBC with a lawsuit, which of course came to nothing, but on a more positive note, it did offer Frances Dee a studio contract and made a similar offer to Sheile Darcy, who plays Lola Montez in the production.

Following completion of *Wells Fargo*, Frank Lloyd was in New York, discussing with newspapermen the impossibility of making further spectacular films such as this because of the expense of hiring extras. "It costs a fortune to employ unskilled labor," he complained. The daily salaries for extras had risen from three dollars a day in the silent era to eight dollars in the late 1930s. According to Lloyd, the daily cost of using extras at the Paramount Ranch, with transportation and meals, was well over $50,000.00.[9] Lloyd's comments did not sit well with everyone, and one trade paper pointed out,

"Of the millions of people who go to the theatres weekly, the greatest number are workers. Most of them either work at low wages or don't work at all. For him, then, to tell these suffering folk that $8 a day for extras, when such extras work probably no more than two days a week, is too much cannot help creating resentment in their hearts. And neither Mr. Lloyd nor any one else in the industry can afford to create such a resentment, particularly when most of them know of the waste that is going on in Hollywood."[10]

One man who would undoubtedly have agreed most sympathetically with the director was Columbia studio head Harry Cohn, who a few years earlier had decided to cut the weekly salaries of his laboratory workers by two dollars a week, down from fourteen to twelve dollars a week.

It was Harry Cohn who hired Lloyd after completion of his final Paramount features, *If I Were King* and *Rulers of the Sea*, for the director's last production of the decade, yet another American historical epic, *The Howards of Virginia*.

Based on the first part of the novel, *The Tree of Liberty*, by Elizabeth Page, and initially intended for release under that title, *The Howards of Virginia* is the story of Matt Howard, a mid 18th Century working-class young man, who marries Jane Peyton, the daughter of a wealthy Williamsburg family, against her parents' wishes. With the support of Thomas Jefferson, Peyton runs for the election in the House of Burgess. He joins the Colonists to fight in the Revolution, is estranged from his wife and son, but eventually reunited. It exploits the dual conflict of a struggle not only against a foreign oppressor, but also, and equally, a fight against the

American Aristocracy and for the right of all people to rule themselves. In a year when war was raging in Europe, the film served as an important reminder to American audiences of their own history, their origins, and their fight for liberty.

At a time of American xenophobia, Louella Parsons summed up what must have been the attitude of many towards the film in her August

Cary Grant and Martha Scott in The Howards of Virginia; *Libby Taylor is seated in rear.*

29, 1941 syndicated column, "I couldn't help thinking as I watched *The Howards of Virginia* how marvelously the studios have risen to the cry for American pictures. This one doesn't need a foreign market, it is an American picture for American people, a history of our country."

To a large extent, *The Howards of Virginia* and earlier *Wells Fargo* are Frank Lloyd's tributes to American history in much the same way as *Cavalcade* was a eulogy to modern British history. With the one, Lloyd paid tribute to the land of his birth, with the other two, he honored his adopted land.

Shot in part on location in Williamsburg, with residents there, along with students from William and Mary College, serving as extras, *The Howards of Virginia* boasted the "most educated extras ever filmed," claimed the studio pressbook. The film began production at the General Service Studio in Hollywood on April 17, 1940, at which time Martha Scott replaced an ailing Joan Fontaine in the female lead. She was subsequently signed to a three-picture contract with Frank Lloyd Productions. Cary Grant was cast as Matt Howard, with Sir Cedric Hardwicke as an impressive Thomas Jefferson. After ten days at the studio, additional scenes were filmed at Santa Cruz, California. Shooting was completed on June 20, 1940, at a reported cost of $1,250,000.00.

Fans of Cary Grant are unenthusiastic about the film, claiming he was "badly miscast," that it was "one of the least successful of Grant's career." And that it "put an end to Grant's unbroken string of box office hits." Perhaps hardest of all for the actor's supporters to take is that it is the first film in which he aged, in which he appeared with gray temples and grown sons.[11]

The Howards of Virginia was a great production for Frank Lloyd to end the decade with. Reviewers were ecstatic in their praise. *The Hollywood Reporter* (August 29, 1940) wrote that "Frank Lloyd has delivered to Columbia the finest picture of his career and one that is bound to find a high place among the meritorious productions of this year…The picture is a triumph for Frank Lloyd…It's the best thing Mr. Lloyd has ever done in his long list of successes." Describing the film as "an able, slow-moving, sincere screen translation" of the Elizabeth Page novel, *Time* (September 16, 1940) continued, "Director Lloyd, who performed a similar service for the British with his 1933 Oscar winner, *Cavalcade*, knows how to dish out history without resorting to a textbook technique. He likes to take a few typical characters of the period, run them through the normal complications of normal people, silhouette them against a background of great dates, deeds, landmarks. Thus he fashioned *The Howards* into a deft exposition of the forces which combined to create the U.S."

Signifying its importance, the film opened in New York at Radio City Music Hall on September 26, 1940. Writing in the *New York Times* the following day, Bosley Crowther commented,

"Seldom do the films illuminate our fundamental ideals with such simple and straightforward analysis as that employed in the present instance; never, to our recollection, has the screen pictured in more magnificent detail the period in American history preceding and including the Revolution. As a record of social progression, the film is a master work…

"As a stern and sobering reminder of our liberal tradition, it is more contemporary than a political speech."

1. Howard Sharpe, "The Star Creators of Hollywood: Frank Lloyd," p. 70.

2. "Director Lloyd Arraigns Exhibitors Who Cut Films," p. 260

3. Story Conference Notes, September 17, 1935, Twentieth Century-Fox Screenplay Collection, Cinema Library, University of Southern California.

4. Quoted in George Geltzer, "Frank Lloyd," pp. 264-265.

5. The Hollywood Reporter, June 29, 1936, p. 3.

6. Quoted in Howard Sharpe, "The Star Creators of Hollywood: Frank Lloyd," p. 102.

7. John R. Woolfenden, "Frank Lloyd Says Time Ripe for 'Great American Film,'" p. C1.

8. Foremost Films of 1938, London: Pitman, 1939, pp. 46-47.

9. "Frank Lloyd's Reasons for Abandoning Big Pictures," p. 204.

10. Daily Variety, April 23, 1940, p. 3.

11. Quotes are taken from Marc Eliot, Cary Grant: A Biography, New York, Harmony Books, p. 208.

CHAPTER EIGHT

The 1940s

A new decade meant a new studio for Frank Lloyd and a return to his filmmaking roots. In the first week of August 1940, the director came back to Universal, where his career had begun in 1913. He was now a semi-independent producer, the head of Frank Lloyd Productions Pictures, Inc., a somewhat unwieldy name compared to that of his unit at Paramount called simply Frank Lloyd Pictures, Inc. The change of name indicated that Lloyd would not necessarily be directing all of the films that his company produced. The plan was to make three films in the 1940-1941 season and a further three titles in the 1941-1942 season.

The first director signed for the new company was Arch Oboler, best known for his work on radio. He was to script and direct *The Flying Yorkshireman*, based on the Eric Knight novel, the screen rights to which Lloyd had owned since 1937, and which Oboler had presented as a radio dramatization, starring Charles Laughton and Elsa Lanchester, on the October 25, 1940 edition of his NBC series, *Every Man's Theatre*. The deal with Oboler fell through, and he did not make his debut as a film director until 1945 and *Bewitched*, based on one of his radio plays; Oboler later gained fame for his 1952 3-D production of *Bwana Devil*. At one point, there were news reports that Chaplin was to star in *The Flying Yorkshireman*, and that Frank Capra and Robert Riskin had offered Lloyd $44,000.00 for the screen rights.

The first production, which Frank Lloyd was also to direct, was initially slated as a sequel to *Mutiny on the Bounty*, but when that fell through, it was announced that Lloyd would begin his new career at Universal with *The Lady from Cheyenne*, starring Carole Lombard. *The Lady from Cheyenne* was indeed Lloyd's first Universal feature, but when it went into production its leading lady was Loretta Young. The film was the first in what was to be, according to the *New York Times* (February 16, 1941), a six-picture deal between Universal and Lloyd's production company, identified by the newspaper as Mayfair Productions (a name which does not appear in the film's credits).

The Lady from Cheyenne took less than two months to film, in January and February 1941, at Universal and on location in Mojave, California, where a Western town set was constructed. It is unusual in that it is a feminist Western, with the heroine, Annie Morgan, fighting for the right, along with other women, to sit on a jury trying the villain, Cork, played by Edward Arnold, and, eventually, persuading the Wyoming legislature to enact women's suffrage. It did — in 1869. Annie's love interest is provided by Steve Lewis, played by Robert Preston, who rescues her from kidnapping by Cork and persuades her to give up politics. *The Lady from Cheyenne* is a surprisingly engaging, romantic Western, with an unusual storyline whose historical background is accurate even if Loretta Young's character did not exactly introduce women's suffrage quite so handily

When the film opened at New York's Roxy Theatre, Bosley Crowther in the *New York Times* (April 18, 1941) admitted, "Frankly, we're slightly disappointed to see Mr. Lloyd turn his hand to such slight fare, but he still displays perfection in the sureness of his directorial touch." For Louella Parsons, writing in her April 1, 1941, syndicated column, *The Lady from Cheyenne* was "an old-fashioned melodrama, made irresistibly funny by having the characters play it straight."

Lloyd's next film should have been a return to form, particularly as it was very definitely a return to a favorite theme, the sea. The director had planned to make *This Woman Is Mine* while under contract to Paramount in 1936, with Claudette Colbert as its star. The project failed to materialize, and Lloyd was able to acquire the rights to the original storyline, a 1932 best-selling novel *I, James Lewis*, by Gilbert Wolf Gabriel from the studio. In all probability, Paramount decided to dispose of the rights because contract director Cecil B. DeMille had announced plans to film another sea-related story, *Reap the Wild Wind*.

Set in 1810, the background to *This Woman Is Mine* concerns the determination of John Jacobs Astor to develop fur trading with the Native Americans of Oregon. He funds a two-year voyage around Cape Horn from New York to the Columbia River, on which Astor sends an unwilling clerk, Robert Stevens. In the most unlikely of casting, Astor is played by Sig Ruman, with Franchot Tone as Stevens, and Broadway musical star Carol Bruce making her screen debut as a female stowaway.

Much of the film, shot between May and July 1941, takes place on board ship, with some location filming at Lake Tahoe, California. Frank Lloyd should have been in his element and should have created a motion picture that would have wide critical appeal. Unfortunately, it did not, with many reviewers comparing it to *Mutiny on the Bounty*, perhaps because of the presence of Franchot Tone and the performance of

Walter Brennan as a Captain Bligh-like captain, and finding it wanting. "Tedious," commented the New York entertainment magazine *Cue*. "It is all very dismal," opined John Mosher in *The New Yorker* (October 18, 1941). In *America* (September 6, 1941), Thomas J. Fitzmorris complained of "too much melodramatic violence." For *Variety* (August 27, 1941), it was "stiff in both script and direction," while Cecelia Ager in *PM* (Octo-

A stunning shot from This Woman Is Mine, *pictorially as beautiful as any to be found in an American silent film.*

ber 13, 1941) labeled it "confused tedium." Even three songs from the leading lady did not help.

Playing hard-bitten Scottish fur traders were two popular character actors, Nigel Bruce and Leo G. Carroll, both of whom it was claimed in publicity were native Scots. In fact, Bruce was born in Mexico, and Carroll in England of Irish parents.

This Woman Is Mine was popular enough with audiences to be reissued in 1949, but under a new and more commercial title, *Fury at Sea*.

From producing and directing in 1941, Lloyd turned to production only in 1942 with three films, *Saboteur*, *The Spoilers* and *The Invisible Agent*. The first is obviously the most important in view of its director, fellow Britisher Alfred Hitchcock. David O. Selznick, to whom Hitchcock was under contract, sold the Hitchcock-John Houseman script to Lloyd, along with the services of the director, for a reported $130,000.00 and ten percent of the gross receipts.[1] In theory, the budget would appear to have been spent on the script and the director, rather than the lackluster stars, Robert Cummings and Priscilla Lane. Hitchcock wanted Gary Cooper for the lead, and Lane was not his choice.

There is no record as to how the two British directors got along. Probably not too well. In his famed interview with Francois Truffaut, Hitchcock was asked if producer Lloyd "used to be a film director." His only response is, "Yes, that's the man."[2] Norman Lloyd (no relation), making his screen debut as the title character villain, states that Frank Lloyd never appeared on the set and that, to the best of his knowledge, he had no input in the filming.[3] Aside from the making of what has to be acknowledged as an entertaining and exciting production, the only good thing to arise from *Saboteur* is the signing of Hitchcock to direct *Shadow of a Doubt* by Lloyd's associate producer on all of these Universal titles, Jack Skirball.

The rights to *The Spoilers* were acquired by Frank Lloyd Productions in November 1941 from agent Charles K. Feldman for $50,000.00 and twenty-five percent of the film's net profits. Only five months earlier, Feldman had purchased the rights for a mere $17,000.00. The Rex Beach novel had previously been filmed in 1914, 1923 and 1930, and would be filmed again, by Universal, in 1955. The star of the original version was Lloyd's old friend and former star William Farnum. The producer cast him here in the role of lawyer Wheaton, a fairly prominent part. William Farnum, whose fame and fortune was long gone, had earlier been cast by Lloyd in *Maid of Salem* and *If I Were King*; brother Franklyn Farnum was cast by Lloyd in *This Woman Is Mine*. There is a certain emotional delight in Frank Lloyd's casting himself as the deputy sheriff who arrests the William Farnum character, particularly as he had played a very similar role in his last screen appearance, in *Les Miserables*. Ray Enright was assigned to direct the 1942 version, with the most important action sequences, the train crash and the gun fight, handled by B. Reeves Eason. Despite the presence of John Wayne and Marlene Dietrich in the leads, the film was only moderately appealing.

Lloyd's final independent production, *The Invisible Agent*, is based on H.G. Wells' *The Invisible Man*, and directed by the generally uninspiring Edwin L. Marin. The storyline has the hero, Jon Hall, possessing the formula for invisibility and thus making himself an ideal American spy in Nazi Germany. During the course of the production, Jack Skirball resigned from his producing partnership with Lloyd and was replaced by George Waggner. Skirball continued at Universal, but Lloyd severed his connections with the studio at this point. "Nobody knows what broke up the producing team of Frank Lloyd and Jack Skirball at Universal, for they made money-making movies," reported Louella Parsons in her May 18, 1942 syndicated column. "And apparently no one is going to find out — because they aren't talking."[4]

With the outbreak of World War Two in Europe and, eventually, America's participation, the British community in Hollywood was anxious to do their "bit" without placing themselves in harm's way. One response was the feature film, *Forever and a Day*. The storyline is concerned with the history of a London home from the 1800s through the blitz. An American reporter in London (Kent Smith) wants to sell the house on behalf of his father, while the British occupant (Ruth Warrick) believes it should be treasured as a living monument to those who lived there. The film closes with the house receiving a direct hit from a Nazi bomb.

The origins of the film are somewhat obscure. It appears to have been based on a story "Let the Rafters Ring" by director Robert Stevenson, then retitled *This Changing World*, and later the storyline was credited to actor Cedric Hardwicke, who served as producer. A vast number of British exiles and others in Hollywood, including seven directors, participated. Lloyd's contribution was direction of the opening and closing scenes. Filming had commenced in May 1941, prior to Pearl Harbor, with revenue promised to be divided between British and American charities. Ultimately, the profits were donated to the National Foundation for Infantile Paralysis.

Forever and a Day was promoted as featuring "78 stars," as well as "42 More Hollywood Favorites," with "21 Famous Writers" and "7 Brilliant Directors." It was all a bit of an exaggeration, and at least one critic, John Mosher in *The New Yorker* (March 20, 1943) commented, "that it's a shame all the stars and all the directors couldn't have got better material out of all the writers."

In 1944, with the rank of major, Lloyd was appointed commanding officer of the 13th Airforce Combat Camera Unit. The director assumed command of a unit that was handicapped by inadequate and obsolete equipment and by its loss of skilled personnel. He set about quickly to rehabilitate the company. One of his sergeants was Jack Sterling, who had worked with Lloyd as a stuntman on *Wells Fargo*. Another recruit from the film industry was a soundman, Lieut. Moran, who covered one of the bombing campaigns by the B-25s, flying out of Guadalcanal. He did not return: "It was his first flight and his last. And when darkness came, I stood in the pouring rain, praying — still hoping."[5]

Unlike other members of the First Motion Picture Unit, fighting World War Two from the safety of the former Hal Roach Studios in

Culver City, to which he was initially assigned, Frank Lloyd spent most of the war on the front lines. Lloyd was not a warmonger in the sense that he supported the ballyhoo of war and attacked men like actor Lew Ayres when he declared himself a pacific and refused to enlist. "Lew Ayres was one of the bravest men I know," recalled the director many years after the close of World War Two. "He had come to hate war. And once

Left to right, director William Seiter, Hannah Dennis, identified as "Colonel of the Women's Division," and Frank Lloyd address a mass studio meeting for the 1942 Community Chest Drive.

he had recognized deep within his soul the futility of war, he refused to kill. This was a man of strong conviction, with the courage to stand pat on it. And by so doing, he showed greater courage than the man with a gun — for he took the same risks unarmed. He served in the front lines, administering to the wounded. Only the very brave could have withstood the criticism heaped upon him at first."[6]

At least one production with which he is credited as director, *Air Pattern — Pacific*, was released by the Office of War Information.

In June 1944, for his work on combat photographic missions in the South Pacific from May 13, 1943 through January 24, 1944, Lloyd was awarded the Legion of Merit by President Roosevelt.

As a civilian, Lloyd returned to Guam in 1946 to serve as coordinator for the Army Air Corps combat camera units in the production of a two-reel Technicolor short subject *The Last Bomb*, released by Warner Bros. The twenty minutes of footage depicted various air raids on Japan from bases in Saipan, Tinian and Guam. The B-29's of the 21st Army Bomber Command were shown taking off, flying through Japanese flak and discharging their bombs. "Top feature of the film," according to *Daily Variety* (October 31, 1946), "is showing of the fighter escort that accompanied

Sylvia Sidney and James Cagney in Blood on the Sun.

the bombers in action against the Japs." The climax, in every sense of the word, of the production was the dropping of the atomic bomb on Nagasaki. It was the first time that color footage of an atomic bomb blast had been shown, and it marked the first time that Frank Lloyd turned from the melodramatics of fiction to the harsher and tragic melodramatics of the real world.

Frank Lloyd's last feature film of the 1940s, and the production with which he anticipated ending his career was *Blood on the Sun*, produced by James Cagney and his brother William, and starring the actor. James and William Cagney had formed Cagney Productions, Inc. in the early 1940s, and *Blood on the Sun* was their second production, following the 1943 release of *Johnny Come Lately*. *Blood on the Sun* marked the fifth time that Cagney had played a newspaperman. The film heralded a comeback for leading lady Sylvia Sidney, who had not been seen on screen since 1941. As a Chinese half-caste, she has an annoying habit of forgetting her Chinese accent. Her role of Iris Hilliard had originally been assigned to Ann Dvorak, who, in all probability, would have been better suited for the part. The role of Tanaka, played in the film by the quietly distinguished John Emery, a model of understatement, was initially to have been portrayed by Orson Welles, who would definitely have been an unsuitable choice.

Filmed at the Samuel Goldwyn Studios in West Hollywood in late 1944, *Blood on the Sun* has as its basis historical fact. As the opening title observes,

"While the entire world watched the early success of the German 'Mein Kampf.' Few were aware of an Oriental Hitler…Baron Giichi Tanaka.

"His plan of world conquest depended upon secrecy for success.

"This story deals with its first exposure by an American newspaperman in Tokyo."

Tanaka was a Japanese politician and general who masterminded that country's expansionist policies in the 1920s, beginning with the takeover of Manchukuo, China. Heavily studio-bound and with fluid camerawork, the film begins outside of the *Tokyo Chronicle*, where crusading reporter Nick Condon (Cagney) has broken the story of the "Tanaka Plan." As Bosley Crowther pointed out in the *New York Times* (June 29, 1945), "Quite contrary to the facts that history tells us." Set in 1929, despite all the American characters wearing 1940s attire, the plot revolves around the Japanese forces, including Tanaka, Colonel Tojo and Captain Oshima, seeking the missing document, which has been stolen by Iris Hilliard, who explains she is making a feminist stand on behalf of Japanese woman who cannot stand up to the militants. She escapes, while Cagney stands up to the "enemy," eventually making it to the American Embassy.

Blood on the Sun is every bit as heavy with racial stereotypes as *A Tale of Two Worlds* from two decades earlier. Smaller roles are played by Orientals (presumably Chinese-Americans only), but all the principal Japanese parts are handled by Caucasian-American actors: John Emery as Tanaka, Robert Armstrong as Colonel Tojo, John Halloran as Captain Oshima, and Leonard Strong as Hijikata. The film does make some, limited attempt to show that there are good Japanese, most notably Prince Tatsugi, played by Frank Puglia, who is opposed to the Tanaka plan and thus assassinated. However, at its release in June 1945, little effort was made to exhibit tolerance towards those responsible for Pearl Harbor. Publicity emphasized that Cagney was "using ju-jitsu on those Japs," urging the audience to "Battle the Japs with Cagney."

The film marks a return to form for Cagney in that it is a typical action feature, very much in the tradition of the actor's 1930s releases from

Warner Bros. Indeed, *The New Yorker* (July 7, 1945) noted that it featured "the most violent workout Mr. Cagney has had since *Public Enemy*." As Cagney explained, "Audiences don't go for torrid love scenes any more — speed and activity are still the most important things in a picture."[7] In a confrontational scene between Cagney and Sidney, the actor yells, "dirty rats," as he learns of Japanese plans to invade the United States once China is subjugated. The actor is first introduced learning ju-jitsu, and then enjoying a Japanese bath as he is confronted by his publisher and the police. The final, lengthy fight sequence is described as "Japanese fashion," and involves a somewhat messy version of Ju-jitsu with Cagney's fighting Oshima, played by John Halloran, who was, in reality, a former police officer and the actor's Judo instructor. "Forgive your enemies — but first get even," is Cagney's philosophy.

The climatic fight is under-cranked to emphasize the speed and ferocity of the encounter. It is also possible that Cagney employs a fight double in some of the shots. The sequence relies only on natural sounds and a melodramatic score. Throughout, the viewer is very much aware of a number of sequences played without dialogue. The most moving of which is undoubtedly the lengthy ritual suicide by Tanaka, which is extremely well choreographed by the director — the real-life Tanaka did indeed die in 1929, taking responsibility for publication of his plan.

Frank Lloyd must have enjoyed directing what is very much an old-fashioned blood-and-thunder melodrama. As Howard Barnes noted in the *New York Herald Tribune* (June 29, 1945) he staged the film "with the broadest strokes imaginable." Aside from the melodramatic plot, there is some great dialogue (presumably the work of soon-to-be-blacklisted Lester Cole), most notably the lines spoken by Tanaka to Tojo in reference to the planned killing of Iris Hillliard:

"Death that comes swiftly is not punishment. There are other forms that are slower, that must be painfully absorbed."

Certainly, *Blood on the Sun* covers a lot of ground, including the murder of an American reporter and his wife (played by Wallace Ford and Rosemary De Camp). "The picture seemed short to me," complained Louella Parsons in her June 23, 1945 syndicated column, "I suppose because it is so fast moving; yet it runs a good hour and a half and every moment of that time is crammed full of excitement and suspense."

Ultimately, as Bosley Crowther noted in the *New York Times*, "we have here an entertaining movie in the time-honored Cagney groove — hard-hitting and explosive, with just enough rudimentary suspense. But let's not approve it too quickly; it treads too boldly upon critical ground. In the first place, it makes a pulpwood fiction out of a historic incident.

And, more than that, it puts the Japs in the popular but highly deceptive 'monkey' class. A true comprehension of our enemies and the sort of people with whom we'll later have to cope is brusquely waylaid by a picture as glibly cocky as *Blood on the Sun*."

It was claimed that the bar seen in the film was an exact replica of that in the Tokyo Imperial Hotel, designed by Frank Lloyd Wright. That might possibly have led in part to the only Academy Award received by *Blood of the Sun* — for Best Art Director – Black-and-White, presented to art director Wiard Ihnen and set decorator A. Roland Fields.

The film received its premiere at the World Security Conference in San Francisco, under the sponsorship of the San Francisco Press Club. It was not particularly well received by either the press or the public, but the film did gross a healthy $800,000.00. Just as it failed to revive Cagney's career, in all probability it persuaded its director that it was time to end his.

1. Donald Spoto, The Dark Side of Genius: The Life of Alfred Hitchcock, Boston: Little, Brown, 1983, p. 251. The film credits Peter Viertel, Joan Harrison and Dorothy Parker for the original script.

2. Hitchcock by Francois Truffaut, New York: Simon and Schuster, 1967, p. 105.

3. Conversation with Anthony Slide, July 4, 2008.

4. According to Frank Lloyd's grandchildren, the breakup was amicable.

5. Frank Lloyd, "Not on the Film Record," unpaged.

6. Ibid.

7. Quoted in pressbook.

CHAPTER NINE

A Farewell to the Screen

After completion of *Blood on the Sun* and *The Last Bomb*, Frank Lloyd decided it was time to retire and enjoy life with his wife, the former Alma Haller, whom he had married thirty-two years earlier. The couple had one daughter, Alma, who had married actor-playwright Franklin Gray in November 1939. (Gray had served as dialogue director on Lloyd's two 1941 films, *The Lady from Cheyenne* and *This Woman Is Mine*, and both he and his wife acted in *If I Were King*) Alma had made her stage debut at the age of eighteen, in June 1934, in a Pasadena Community Playhouse production of *Cavalcade*; she made her Broadway debut in 1935 in George Bernard Shaw's *The Simpleton of the Unexpected Isles*. Lloyd shelved a projected film with Charles Laughton, and moved to a new home, the Shannon Water Ranch in California's Carmel Valley. "He wants to get into blue jeans and work from dawn to dark on his ranch," reported a local newspaper. "He'll plow the alfalfa field under this year and plant potatoes."[1]

Frank Lloyd might have remained in retirement had it not been for the death of his wife Alma on March 16, 1952, at the age of fifty-eight.[2] Rather than continue at the ranch without her, Lloyd decided to return to direction. "Frank now realizes that work is the best solace," reported loyal friend and supporter Louella Parsons in her April 24, 1952 syndicated column. In February 1953, Lloyd signed to make two feature films a year at Republic Pictures under a two-year contract, one of a handful of major names — including John Ford, Frank Borzage, Lewis Milestone, and Fritz Lang — who directed briefly at the studio which was borderline "poverty row" and borderline major producer. The *Los Angeles Times* (May 10, 1953) noted that *Cavalcade* had been made in the midst of the depression and that the industry was facing another crisis in the competition from television: "The fact that Frank Lloyd will again be making pictures is an interesting commentary on the present movie age. Hollywood can still rely on its veterans, especially directors." *Daily Variety* (February 11, 1953) considered Lloyd's return to the screen worthy of a front-page story.

"I consider it an honor to have Frank Lloyd, one of the truly great direc-

Edmond O'Brien and Ruth Roman in Shanghai Story.

tors of the motion picture industry, associated with Republic," announced studio head Hebert J. Yates. However, Lloyd's terms were not as generous as those of his fellow directors; he was paid $9,800.00 for each film, along with twenty-five percent of the net profits.

The director's first production at Republic was *The Shanghai Story*, a drama of spying in Shanghai after the Communist takeover of China, written by Seton I. Miller and Steve Fisher from a story by Lester Yard. The plot centers around a group of individuals, of various nationalities, led by Ruth Roman and Edmond O'Brien, interned in one of the city's hotels. Despite being completed in December 1953, *The Shanghai Story* was not released until November of the following year — an ominous sign which trade paper reviews confirmed. *The Hollywood Reporter* (November 26, 1954) described the film as "a routine meller, overlong and over-talky." *Daily Variety* (September 27, 1954) commented, "Frank Lloyd, who seems to have had an off-day on this one, seldom gets a ring of realism into performances of most cast members, probably due to the stock story he was faced with."

When *The Shanghai Story* opened at New York's Palace Theatre on September 24, 1954, the second-string critic for the *New York Times*, Oscar

Richard Carlson as William Travis and Ben Cooper as Jeb Lacey in The Last Command.

Godbout, was scathing. "Balderdash. And cheap balderdash to boot," he proclaimed. "The director, Frank Lloyd, has made some fine films in the past, *Cavalcade* and *Mutiny on the Bounty*, among others. It is to be hoped that he will again. However, with *The Shanghai Story*, he merely went through the motions, and badly at that." Unfortunately, the *New York Times* did not even bother to review the next film, superior as it obviously was.

More to Lloyd's liking and more in the Lloyd tradition is *The Last Command*, which began filming at Republic on March 1, 1955, under the working title of *The Texas Legionnaires*, and was released, six months later, on August 5 of that year. It is the story of Jim Bowie (played by Sterling Hayden), and the secession of Texas from Mexico, leading up to the fall of the Alamo. In a relatively small role is Arthur Hunnicutt as an older, bearded Davy Crockett, most unlike Fess Parker who had starred as the character at the same time in two Disney films. Here was a film that John Wayne had wished to star in for Republic, but he had left the studio and he was not to make his own, independent production until 1960.

The Last Command, with a negative cost of over two million dollars, was Republic's highest budgeted film. It boasted an often intrusive score by Max Steiner, including the song "Jim Bowie," which is of the period in which the film was made rather than the period in which the film is set, sung by Gordon MacRae. As had been happening more and more with Lloyd's films since the 1930s, the direction of the action scenes was assigned to another, in this case veteran Republic filmmaker William Witney.

As befitted the epic, it was billed as shot in Republic's two-color process, Trucolor, which was far from true to its titular claim, but here does not look at all bad.[3] *The Last Command* was Frank Lloyd's last feature film, and the only one shot entirely in color, ironic in that he had commented, "Color! I hold no brief for it, you know.

"Life itself is in black and white — shades and hues are a detriment to a good portrayal. The public wants color with a mood, not a visual illusion done by a mechanical contrivance. The audience colors a scene for itself — the way it wants it."[4]

Despite approximately one month of location shooting in Texas, at Bracketville and nearby Fort Clark, the film is studio-bound, and the dialogue (by Warren Duff from a story by Sy Bartlett) is often stilted and over-laden with historical narrative. Happily, Sterling Hayden leads a stellar cast, delivering a quiet undemonstrative and appealing performance. Frank Lloyd's direction is, as always, workmanlike, and occasionally innovative as, for example, when an overhead shot of a decanter and wine glasses is used to illustrate the passage of time as Hayden as Bowie and J. Carrol Naish as Santa Anna drink and talk.

"It was one of Sterling Hayden's best pictures because of Frank," asserts Ernest Borgnine. "*The Last Command* was no easy production. It was a tough, hard picture to make, but there was no yelling at all. Frank was not that kind of man."[5] Sterling Hayden would claim that he took this all-American role "to atone" for an earlier brush with Communism.[6]

The Last Command was given its world premiere at the Majestic Theatre, San Antonio, Texas, on August 3, 1955, with Frank Lloyd and others in attendance. Reviews were positive, with *Newsweek* (October 3, 1955) describing the film as "Americana without flags," and *The Hollywood Reporter* (July 21, 1955) calling it "a big lavish screen spectacle that is aglitter with bright pageantry." Despite the film's positive reviews and relative commercial success, Frank Lloyd was not asked to remain at

Republic. The studio itself was close to the end of its life, and the director's next film, *Papa Married a Mormon*, for which he was to have been paid $60,000.00 was cancelled.

Frank Lloyd was, in all probability, unconcerned with the end of his Republic period and his return to retirement. In 1954, he had met divorced screenwriter Virginia Kellogg, almost twenty years his junior, at

Ernest Borgnine as settler Mike Radin in The Last Command.

the home of fellow writer Robert Carson. Kellogg was a charter member of the Screen Writers Guild and a member of its board of directors from 1951-1953; she had received two Academy Award nominations, for *White Heat* (1949) and *Caged* (1950). After returning from a promotional tour for *The Last Command* in the United Kingdom, Lloyd telephoned Kellogg and asked her to marry him. She agreed, and the couple was wed on a yacht as it passed under San Francisco's Golden Gate Bridge on September 2, 1955. Not only did Lloyd decide upon permanent retirement from direction, but also his wife announced that she was giving up her own career to be Mrs. Frank Lloyd

The couple remained happily married until Frank Lloyd's death, in Los Angeles, on August 10, 1960. His Christian Science funeral service at Forest Lawn was attended by a vast number of major Hollywood figures. Active pallbearers included John Ford, Joel McCrea, Antonio Moreno, Gene Raymond, George Sidney, and Howard Strickland. Honorary pallbearers included Lew Ayres, Frank Borzage, Frank Capra, Gary Cooper, Bing Crosby, Walt Disney, Cary Grant, Charles Laughton, Joseph M. Schenck, and Randolph Scott.

Virginia Kellogg remarried in 1963 — to retired railroad executive Albert Mortenseen — and died, in Los Angeles, on April 8, 1981, at the age of seventy-three.

It would be pleasing to record that following Frank Lloyd's death, there was a resurgence of interest in his work. Sadly, such is not the case. Even with the growth of enthusiasm for virtually every aspect of motion picture history, however unimportant and irrelevant, the name of Frank Lloyd has been overlooked. It is ironic that at the 1934 Academy Awards presentation, it was Frank Lloyd who received the trophy and Frank Capra who was humiliated. Eighty years later, it is Lloyd who suffers the humiliation of being forgotten, while Capra remains in high regard.

During his lifetime, despite the magnitude of his films, Lloyd was never much of a self-promoter. It was the merchandise (the films themselves) that was important, rather than the manufacturer.

In a way, it must be admitted that there is no Lloyd style. Everything is very good, very orderly, very professional, and very much a credit to whatever studio the director was under contract. He was a company director — and proud of it. *The Times* (London) acknowledged this in its August 12, 1960 obituary:

"His work was all of a high professional standard, but so varied in form and content as to make it difficult to point to anything which could be regarded as distinctively his. He had a flair for handling action sequences and an enjoyment of colorful period backgrounds and full-blooded drama. He was an excellent technician who made several outstanding films — and when the films are of the quality of *Mutiny on the Bounty* or *Cavalcade* that is no mean achievement."

Frank Lloyd was never the stereotypical director, with the temperament and arrogance of a Josef von Sternberg, megaphone in hand and clothing that was autocratic in style and appearance. As one writer put it at the height of the director's fame, he looked like a respectable greengrocer or a high-class dentist or a man selling insurance. "He doesn't look like what you think a director ought to look like. He wears dark blue clothes and, no fooling, he wears 'em. When going into action on the set, he first removes his dark blue coat and that reveals him in a dark blue shirt and a dark blue necktie and dark blue trousers and a dark blue cap.

"As he slowly works into the day's chore, he removes his necktie, crumples it into a ball and stuffs it into his pocket, thereby ruining one tie. If the scene is fearfully intense, he is likely to have the directorial jitters and begin moving lamps around or sweeping imaginary dust off objects at hand, or shoving lights this way or that. The way you can tell if he is inwardly wrought up over a stubborn or exciting scene, he quits smoking cigarettes. Most people smoke if excited or jammed up, but he quits."[7]

Just as one looks in vain for references to Frank Lloyd in most major published film sources through the years, one finds incredibly little on the internet. It seems that Google is familiar with architect Frank Lloyd Wright, but not director Frank Lloyd. The architect of so many classic films is truly forgotten.

There was a small and noble effort to honor the director in his native land with the 1997 publication of E. Mark McLachlan's *"A Top Notcher": Frank Lloyd, Scotland's Triple Oscar Winner*. It is unfortunate that the title gets it so wrong — Lloyd won only two Academy Awards! However, the author does make the very valid point that "Frank Lloyd *is* the History of the Cinema."[8]

Admittedly, Frank Lloyd's feature films have fared well in terms of preservation. In Los Angeles, the UCLA Film and Television Archive has preserved and restored a number, and they have become something of a mainstay in the Archive's biennial preservation festival.[9] In 1973, a 35mm print of the long lost *Oliver Twist* was found in Yugoslavia, restored and presented at the Los Angeles International Film Festival (Filmex) in the presence of its star, Jackie Coogan. It took thirty-five years for his native Glasgow to remember Lloyd with a screening of *Oliver Twist* at the local festival in February 2008. The organizers "organized" a piano accompaniment for the film, not even a trio let alone an orchestra, and claimed, a third of a century too late, that it was recently restored. "It is a shame that he is not better known in his native land," said the festival co-director. Dishonored in Scotland might be a more potent comment.[10]

1. "No More Schedules for Frank Lloyd: He's Turned Carmel Valley Farmer," Monterey Peninsula Herald, November 11, 1946.

2. Some modern sources list an earlier wife, Dorothy Cummings. Could this be the actress and screenwriter Dorothy Cumming, who appears in The Divine Lady? If so, she is much too young to have married Frank Lloyd prior to Alma Haller.

3. In reality, this late in the studio's history, its films might have been promoted as shot in Trucolor, but actually they were filmed in the far superior Eastmancolor.

4. Howard Sharpe, "The Star Creators of Hollywood: Frank Lloyd," p. 104.

5. Ernest Borgnine in an interview with Anthony Slide, August 6, 2002.

6. Frank Thompson, Alamo Movies, East Berlin, Pa.: Old Mill Books, 1991.

7. Frank Condon, "Mutiny on the Set," p. 67.

8. P. 3.

9. Robert Gitt of the UCLA Film and Television Archive has preserved and/or restored a large number of Lloyd's films, beginning with The Reform Candidate and Madame La Presidente, and including The Sea Hawk, The Divine Lady, Weary Wiver, and Servant's Entrance.

10. Quoted in Brian Pendreigh and Gavin Madeley, "Scotland 1st Oscar Winner," p. 47.

BIBLIOGRAPHY

(Any references fully annotated in the footnotes are not listed here)

"Art Only Incentive in Films," *Los Angeles Times*, March 11, 1923, Section III, p. 15.

Bodeen, DeWitt, "Henry James into Film," *Films in Review*, March 1977, pp. 163-170.

Bratton, Jacky, Jim Cook and Christine Gledhill, ed. *Melodrama: Stage, Picture, Screen*. London: British Film Institute, 1994.

"Breath of the 'Briny' in Sea Productions," *New York Times*, June 8, 1924, p. X10.

Brownlow, Kevin. *The Parade's Gone By*. New York: Alfred A. Knopf, 1968.

"Camera in the Desert," *New York Times*, February 2, 1936, p. X4.

"Case History of Metro's 'Mutiny,'" *New York Times*, November 3, 1935, p. X4.

Collins, Keith, "Brit Helmer Oscar Trivia," *Daily Variety*, December 6, 2006, p. A16.

Coward, Noel. *Collected Plays*. London: Methuen, 1979.

Day, Barry. *Coward on Film: The Cinema of Noel Coward*. Lanham, Md.: Scarecrow Press, 2005.

"Director Lloyd Arraigns Exhibitors Who Cut Films," *The Moving Picture World*, January 10, 1920, p. 260.

Durling, E.V., "A Director with a Conscience," *Photoplay*, July 1917, pp. 91-92.

Elwood, Muriel. *Pauline Frederick: On and Off the Stage*. Chicago: A. Kroch, 1940.

Frank, Sam. *Ronald Colman: A Bio-Bibliography*. Westport, Ct.: Greenwood Press, 1997.

"Frank Lloyd," in John Wakeman, ed. *World Film Directors: Volume 1: 1890-1945*. New York: H.W. Wilson Company, 1987, pp. 683-688.

"Frank Lloyd Scores," *The Moving Picture World*, December 18, 1915, p. 2158.

"Frank Lloyd Series for First National," *The Moving Picture World*, June 9, 1923, p. 511.

"Frank Lloyd Signs Arch Oboler to 2-Way Term Deal," *Daily Variety*, September 30, 1940, p. 4.

"Frank Lloyd's Reasons for Abandoning Big Pictures," *Harrison's Reports*, December 18, 1937, p. 204.

"Frank Lloyd's U Pict. On Capt. Bligh's Life," *Daily Variety*, May 18, 1940.

franklloydfilms.com

Frischkorn, Craig, "Frank Lloyd's Berkeley Square (1933): Re-adapting Henry James's The Sense of the Past," *Literature/Film Quarterly*, vol. XXVIII, no. 1, 2000, pp. 7-11.

Gehman, Geoff. *Down But Not Quite Out in Hollow-Weird: A Documentary in Letters of Eric Knight*. Lanham, Md.: Scarecrow Press, 1998.

Geltzer, George, "Frank Lloyd," *Films in Review*, May 1981, pp. 257-274.

Gledhill, Christine, ed. *Home Is Where the Heart Is: Studies in Melodrama and the Woman's Film*. London: British Film Institute, 1987.

"Good Story Absolutely Necessary to Successful Photo Plays, Says Frank Lloyd," *The Universal Weekly*, June 5, 1915, p. 15.

Hagopian, Kevin, "Declarations of Independence: A History of Cagney Productions," *The Velvet Light Trap*, no. 22, 1986, pp. 16-32.

Hanson, Patricia King, ed. *The American Film Institute Catalog of Motion Pictures Produced in the United States: Feature Films, 1911-1920*. Berkeley: University of California Press, 1988.

_____. *The American Film Institute Catalog of Motion Pictures Produced in the United States: Feature Films, 1931-1940*. Berkeley: University of California Press, 1993.

_____. *The American Film Institute Catalog of Motion Pictures Produced in the United States: Feature Films, 1941-1950*. Berkeley: University of California Press, 1999.

Harris, Warren G. *Clark Gable: A Biography*. New York: Harmony Books, 2002.

Hockman, Stanley, ed. *American Film Directors: A Library of Film Criticism*. New York: Frederick Ungar, 1974.

Kracauer, Siegfried. *Theory of Film: The Redemption of Physical Reality*. New York: Oxford University Press, 1960.

Lewis, Mildred, "Frank Lloyd," *Camera!*, vol. II, no. 39, January 10, 1920, p. 6.

Lloyd, Frank, "Slapped by the Ocean," *Photoplay*, June 1914, p. 132.

_____. *An Outline of the History of Drama*. Hollywood: Palmer Photoplay Corporation, 1922 (included as section seven, vol. II of Palmer's Handbook).

_____, "In the Tomorrow of Film Production," in Laurence A. Hughes, ed., *The Truth about the Movies*. Hollywood: Hollywood Publishers, 1924, pp. 356-358.

_____, "Publicity and Exploitation," *Motion Picture Director*, vol. I, no. 11, May 1925, pp. 7, 19.

_____, as told to Virginia Kellogg. *With the Tide*. Unpublished, sixty-one page manuscript. Origin Unknown.

_____, "Hollywood, Get Courageous," *The Hollywood Reporter*, 6th annual directors' edition, June 8, 1936, pp..29, 71.

_____, "Hollywood's Silliest Question – 'What Kind of a Story Do You Want?'" *The Hollywood Reporter*, 8th anniversary edition, October 24, 1938, pp. II, VIII.

_____, "Not on the Film Record," *The Hollywood Reporter*, 23rd anniversary edition, October 26, 1953, unpaged.

Lonergan, Elizabeth, "Directors I Have Met," *Pictures and Picturegoer*, February 1923, p. 39.

McLachlan, E Mark. *"A Top Notcher": Frank Lloyd, Scotland's Triple Oscar Winner*. Glasgow: Scottish Screen, 1997.

Mercer, John and Martin Shingler. *Melodrama: Genre, Style, Sensibility*. London: Wallflower, 2004.

Munden, Kenneth W., ed. *The American Film Institute Catalog of Motion Pictures Produced in the United States: Feature Films, 1921-1930*. New York: R.R. Bowker, 1971.

"Mutiny on the Bounty," *Stage*, May 1936, pp. 44-45.

"Needed – a Soul to Fix Future of the Camera," *New York Times*, May 11, 1924, Section VIII, p. 4.

"New Frank Lloyd Firm Moving to Universal," *Daily Variety*, June 21, 1940, p. 6.

"Otis Turner: Dean of Universal Motion Picture Directors," *The Universal Weekly*, September 5, 1914, pp. 8, 12.

"Otis Turner Dies," *The Moving Picture World*, April 20, 1918, p. 377.

"Own Work Reflects Spirit of Directors," *The Moving Picture World*, July 12, 1919, pp. 214-215.

"Pallas Pictures to Make Debut," *The Moving Picture World*, October 30, 1915, p. 945.

Parish, Robert. *Growing up in Hollywood*. New York: Harcourt Brace Jovanovich, 1976.

Pendreigh, Brian. "Scotland's 1st Oscar Winner," *Daily Mail* [London], February 9, 2008, p.47.

Penfield, Cornelia, "Hollywood Helmsman," *Stage*, May 1936, pp. 52-53.

"Rafael Sabatini," www.wikipedia.org.

"Quotes by Rafael Sabatini," www.goodreads.com.

Ramsaye, Terry, "Cavalcade as seen at the Gaiety Theatre, New York," *Motion Picture Herald*, January 14, 1931, p. 16.

Rulers of the Sea, *Photoplay Studies*, vol. V, no. 19, series of 1939.

Sarris, Andrew. *The American Cinema: Directors and Directions, 1929-1968*. New York: E.P. Dutton, 1968.

The Sea Hawk, www.moviediva.com.

Semenov, Lillian Wurtzel and Carla Winter, ed. *William Fox, Sol M. Wurtzel and the Early Fox Film Corporation: Letters, 1917-1923*. Jefferson, N.C.: McFarland, 2001.

Service, Faith, "Frank Lloyd's Jackie Coogan," *Motion Picture Classic*, vol. XVI, no. 4, June 1923, pp. 42-43.

Sharpe, Howard, "The Star Creators of Hollywood: Frank Lloyd," *Photoplay*, vol. L, no. 5, November 1936, pp. 70-71, 101-104.

Spicer, Christopher J. *Clark Gable: Biography, Filmography, Bibliography*. Jefferson, N.C.: McFarland, 2002.

Stenn, David. *Clara Bow: Running Wild*. New York: Cooper Square Press, 2000.

Sternberg, Josef von. *Fun in a Chinese Laundry*. New York: Macmillan, 1965.

Varconi, Victor and Ed Honeck. *It's Not Enough to Be Hungarian*. Denver: Graphic Impressions, 1976.

Vardac, A. Nicholas. *Stage to Screen: Theatrical Method from Garrick to Griffith*. Cambridge, Ma.: Harvard University Press, 1949.

Variety Film Reviews: 1907-1980. New York: Garland Publishing, 1985.

Woolfenden, John R., "Frank Lloyd Says Time Ripe for 'Great American Film,'" *Los Angeles Times*, May 10, 1936, p. C1.

APPENDIX A

"Slapped by the Ocean"

This short anecdotal piece was published as part of a series. It is of interest as the first in print by Frank Lloyd, written just as he becomes a director; Captain Kidd *dates from 1913 and* Won in the Clouds *from 1914. The last nine words are so typical of Frank Lloyd's approach to filmmaking.*

In a scene for *Captain Kidd* I was pitched from the rigging of a large ship into the ocean. The fall was 45 feet, and, being thrown out by three husky sailors, made it more interesting. The rush through the air was very thrilling and the landing in a spread-eagle attitude was more than thrilling. For two weeks I had a black eye, caused by having the ocean hit me unprepared. Needless to say, we did not get a "still" photograph of the fall.

In a recent feature, called *Won in the Clouds*, I took a chance and stayed ten feet back of Kaffir hut which was blown up with a large charge of powder. In the scene it looked as though I were in the hut when it was dynamited, for I came forward out of the falling debris and smoke, stumbled within ten feet of the camera and collapsed. I was dead for a whole afterwards, but we got the picture, which is the important thing.

(Reprinted from Photoplay, *June 1914, p. 132)*

APPENDIX B

"In the Tomorrow of Film Production"

This and the next piece by Frank Lloyd are reprinted here as typical of a number essays by the director. Those in which he discusses specific productions of his own are generally quoted within the main body of the text (and referenced in the bibliography), but these articles stand alone as what may perhaps best be described as "think pieces." Here, Lloyd returns to a favorite theme, the need to recruit screen actors from the stage, or, more accurately, from theatrical stock companies. Perhaps the "songs" of which he writes are represented by The Sea Hawk *and the "symphonies" of the future by* Mutiny on the Bounty. *In many areas, this piece is very similar to an interview that Frank Lloyd gave to the* New York Times, *and published on May 11, 1924, under the heading of "Needed — A Soul to Fix Future of the Cinema."*

What will be the next advance in screen productions; who will make it — how will it be made? Often has the question been asked and many different answers have been returned, but to me there is but one answer — Motion pictures must be given a soul.

Whereas in the past, spectacle, technical novelty, elaboration, and mechanical effect have brought about our greatest triumph, in the future, progress must be made by artistry, understanding, study, and careful hard work. Where we have been creating "songs" in the past we must create "symphonies" in the future. Where we have been "tricksters" and "assemblers" in the past we must be real "spiritualists" and "artists" in the tomorrow of film production. And by "we" I mean producers, directors, actors, authors, technicians — every one interested in the preparation of a film play for the public.

The novelty of motion pictures is gone. We must not make attending the theatre in the future a fad or a habit; we must make our productions compel interest.

In five years the art of photography has developed more than in sixty-five years previously. Studio lighting has reached the point that it justifies recognition as a distinct science. Studio properties have become so perfect that they deceive expert craftsmen; we have miniaturized aeroplane wrecks and ship disasters, duplicated perfectly some of the finest architectural achievements in history and we have made artificial spider webs. At a moment's notice we have injected spectacular incidents into weak scenarios and we have manufactured thrills, suspense and romance to fit the occasion. In fear that our idea might not hit the mark we have exaggerated life and we have missed the sweetness, the delicacy, the sugar-fine fabric which is real life, truly impressive and thoroughly satisfying to behold. There have been a few pictures which will always live as masterpieces of dramatic and cinematic achievement, but too few. The future success in studio work depends on those who know their subject, not think they know it; those who observe, study and accurately interpret; our pictures must be a part of us; we must not manufacture a story to match our weakness — we must build our strength to match good stories.

Indeed the greatest advancement that can be recorded in the future history of the screen will be noted in giving the motion picture a soul — that inspirational depth it has little know before and cannot progress without.

Who will advance the art of the screen?

Every man and woman interested in the making of a motion picture must do his or her full share.

The author must write well about subjects he knows intimately. It isn't necessary to have a train wreck, an automobile chase, a half dozen murders, million dollar settings in every story. But stories must have sincerity, a clearly defined moral, must accurately describe life — there must be a genius visible in the network of every theme. One real good situation may be sufficient to make a story an immortal triumph if it has quality — not just quantity of dramatic incident.

The producer must assist the creators of screen plans by allowing sufficient time to make pictures correctly. No great masterpiece of art has ever been made according to a time-clock. Money must not regulate a picture's greatness. One story may cost a million dollars and another equally as impressive only fifty thousand. The producer must select his story wisely and his directors and actors carefully. The producer must encourage new ideas, new methods; not establish a hard and fast rule which prohibits the progress of art.

Perhaps the greatest advance the screen is to know must come from the actor. The actor must actually live his part, however small; he must know his character. He must not be visibly acting, his every gesture must be natural, typical and accurate. He must have poise.

Today there are too few actors in the studio, which accounts for a few so-called stars appearing in so many pictures; even the best of them have become more like machines than real people. But, until the screen can obtain new talent (not just new faces) for its histrionical [sic] duties, its progress is bound to be very slow. There are too many actors and actresses on the screen today who have become successful because they are "types" rather than "artists," which condition is responsible for so many changes in the popularity and commercial value of some players and the steady increase in the success of others.

The best acting talent today is in the stock companies, where one actor must play many different roles, must become intimate with many different characters, must study every day and must make his success by his knowledge of many things not of just one particularly type.

A motion picture is only made once. The actor of the future must have experience enough to supply any number of moods and characters upon call. In the past we have been more concerned about an actor looking his part than we have in his acting his part. In the future the demand will be the reverse and appearance will be secondary to understanding.

(Reprinted from Laurence A. Hughes, ed., The Truth about the Movies, *Hollywood: Hollywood Publishers, Inc., 1924, pp. 356-358)*

APPENDIX C

"Hollywood, Get Courageous"

Here, Frank Lloyd comments on some films which he did not direct but which have impressed him for various reasons. The writing style is very down-to-earth and far removed from the somewhat academic approach that Lloyd used in earlier pieces.

Courage is pulling the picture industry over the hump.

Because there are men brave enough to junk old outworn superstitions, bogies and fetishes; test new tacks and new ideas, and spend money in times when money was tight, Hollywood now finds itself on the threshold of one of the greatest eras in its history.

During the past two years, new formulae of picture making have been bursting over the film world like fireworks on a dark night, and a delighted public has shown its appreciation by increased box office returns.

It took courage to make such pictures as *Lives of a Bengal Lancer*, *Louis Pasteur*, and *The Informer*. Every one was a so-called "big" production, and cost a lot of money. In a way, each was a gamble because it deviated from the beaten path and defied "don'ts" which had been religiously observed by producers for years. But the returns they brought proved how shrewd the gamblers were.

It used to be an axiom in this industry that every picture needed a strong love story. But that was before *The Lancer*. Here was a romance of adventure — and with the hero killed at the end, too. Sheer madness! But the artistry with which it was done put it over. It cleaned up.

Louis Pasteur was another departure. The story of a man and his dreams. A romance of science, with the human love story decidedly secondary. And the public loved it.

The Trail of the Lonesome Pine, with its advanced color technique, was another seven league stride. Paramount made it, and now every studio in the industry has become color conscious. Three or four of them already have color films in preparation. But *The Informer* was perhaps the biggest surprise of them all.

This picture with its stark Dublin background, its story of a thick-headed Irish Iscariot, its overtones of doom, was forecast for failure by most of the "experts" from the very preview. They said it was "artistic," and to them that was enough to damn it.

But it fooled 'em. It proved to their amazement that such things can be turned to gold if you have the touch.

The movies, certainly, are coming of age.

Imagine what would have happened so short a time as two years ago if a director had suggested bringing Shakespearean tragedy to the screen? Hollywood would have though him crazy — or "artistic," which meant practically the same thing.

But today *Romeo and Juliet* is considered by MGM as worthy of over a million dollar production.

Every picture, as a matter of fact, is a "Big" picture if attacked with enthusiasm, vigor and intelligence. The amount of money and number of people in the cast doesn't weigh the entertainment value or the box office draw. *It Happened One Night* is a good case in point.

There isn't a producer, director or exhibitor in the business who hasn't had the experience of starting with something he thought was "Big," only to have it phff out like a wet match, and then have a so-called program picture hit the bull's eye of public appeal and surprise him.

By this time Hollywood has learned, at the cost of some rather bitter experience, that the picture market has grown selective. Pictures that sell have to be good.

As a result the search for talent has become intensified.

Competition is keen, standards are high, and from the way the red corpuscles are popping I look for still further advancement in every phase of the industry.

(Reprinted from The Hollywood Reporter, *6th annual directors' number, June 8, 1936, pp. 29, 71)*

APPENDIX D

Filmography

At the start of his career at Universal, Frank Lloyd claimed to have made more than fifty films in one year. This filmography is thus in all probability incomplete for the period 1914-1915, credit information for which is taken primarily from *The Universal Weekly*.

AS AN ACTOR AT UNIVERSAL

All films are one- or two-reel short subjects unless otherwise indicated.

1913

Genesis IV – 9 (unconfirmed), *Captain Kidd* (3 reels), *The Madonna of the Slums*, *The Buccaneers* (three reels, also screenplay).

1914

Shadows of Life, *The She Wolf*, *Under the Black Flag*, *The Dead Line*, *For the Freedom of Cuba*, *One of the Bravest*, *The Law of His Kind*, *Unjustly Accused* (also screenplay), *Captain Jenny, S.A.* (three reels), *By Radium's Rays*, *Won in the Clouds*, *The Mexican's Last Raid*, *On Suspicion*, *Dangers of the Veldt* (three reels), *The Test*, *Stolen Glory*, *The Last of Their Race* (also known as *The Feud*), *On the Verge of War* (three reels), *The Spy* (four reels), *The Woman in Black*, *On the Rio Grande*, *The Love Victorious* (three reels), *Prowlers of the Wild*, *The Sob Sister*, *Circle 17*, *Through the Flames*, *A Prince of Bavaria*, *As the Wind Blows*, *Kid Regan's Hands*, *The Opened Shutters* (four reels), *Damon and Pythias* (six reels).

1915

The Black Box (15-episode serial; in episode three, "The Pocket Wireless," only).

AS A DIRECTOR

1914

The Law of His Kind. Universal/Rex. Two reels. Screenplay: Philip Walsh. With Herbert Rawlinson, Cleo Madison, Frank Lloyd.

As the Wind Blows. Universal/Rex. Two reels. With William Worthington, Herbert Rawlinson, Anna Little.

The Vagabond. Universal/Rex. Two reels. Screenplay: Ruth Ann Baldwin. With William Worthington, Frank Lloyd, Helen Wright, Herbert Rawlinson.

The Link That Binds. Universal/Rex. Two reels. Screenplay: Frank Lloyd and Philip Walsh. With William Worthington, Herbert Rawlinson, Frank Lloyd.

The Chorus Girl's Thanksgiving. Universal/Rex. Two reels. Screenplay: James Dayton. With Anna Little, Herbert Rawlinson, William Worthington, Frank Lloyd.

Traffic in Babies. Universal/Rex. One reel. Screenplay: Ruth Ann Baldwin. With Herbert Rawlinson, Beatrice Van, Helen Wright, Frank Lloyd.

A Page from Life. Universal/Rex. Two reels. Screenplay: Frank Lloyd. With Anna Little, Herbert Rawlinson, Frank Lloyd.

1915

Pawns of Fate. Universal/Rex. Two reels. Screenplay: Frank Lloyd, based on a story by Ruth Ann Baldwin. With Marc Robbins, Frank Lloyd, George Larkin, Gretchen Lederer.

The Temptation of Edwin Swayne. Universal/Rex. Two reels. Screenplay: Ruth Ann Baldwin. With Frank Lloyd, George Larkin, Gretchen Lederer.

Wolves of Society. Universal/Rex. Two reels. Screenplay: Frank Lloyd. With Helen Leslie, Frank Lloyd, Marc Robbins, Harry Millarde.

His Last Serenade. Universal/Laemmle. One reel. Screenplay: James Dayton. With Frank Lloyd, Helen Leslie, Gretchen Lederer.

Martin Lowe, Financier. Universal/Laemmle. One reel. With Frank Lloyd, Gretchen Lederer, Helen Leslie.

An Arrangement with Fate. Universal/Laemmle. One reel. Screenplay: Ruth Ann Baldwin. With Frank Lloyd, George Larkin, Gretchen Lederer.

To Redeem an Oath. Universal/Laemmle. Two reels. Screenplay: James Dayton. With Frank Lloyd, Millard K. Wilson, Olive Golden.

The Bay of Seven Isles. Universal/Laemmle. One reel. Screenplay: James Dayton. With Frank Lloyd, Helen Leslie, Marc Robbins.

His Last Trick. Universal/Laemmle. One reel. Screenplay: Frank Lloyd. With Millard K. Wilson, Duke Worne, Helen Leslie.

The Pinch. Universal/Laemmle. Two reels. Screenplay: Frank Lloyd. With Millard K. Wilson, Gretchen Lederer, Frank Lloyd.

His Captive. Universal/Laemmle. Two reels. Screenplay: Helen Bailey. With Frank Lloyd, Marc Robbins, Millard K. Wilson, Gretchen Lederer.

Life's Furrow. Universal/Laemmle. One reel. Screenplay: George Edwardes Hill. With Millard K. Wilson, Helen Leslie.

When the Spider Tore Loose. Universal/Laemmle. Screenplay: Frank Lloyd and William M. Caldwell. With Frank Lloyd, Millard K. Wilson, Olive Golden.

Nature's Triumph. Universal/Laemmle. One reel. With Frank Lloyd, Helen Leslie, Charles Alexander. (Also known as *The Cure of the Mountains*)

A Prophet of the Hills. Universal/Laemmle. Two reels. Screenplay: James Dayton. With Frank Lloyd, Helen Leslie, Marc Robbins.

$100,000. Universal/Laemmle. One reel. Screenplay: Frank Lloyd. With Frank Lloyd, Helen Leslie, Mildred Adams.

The Little Girl of the Attic. Universal/Laemmle. Two reels. Screenplay: Calder Johnstone. With William Canfield, Millard K. Wilson, Helen Leslie.

The Toll of Youth. Universal/Laemmle. One reel. Screenplay: Earl Hewitt, based on a story by Donald Meany. With Marc Robbins, Millard K. Wilson, Helen Leslie.

Fate's Alibi. Universal/Laemmle. One reel. Screenplay: Frank Lloyd, based on a story by C.W. Fassett. With Helen Leslie, Millard K. Wilson, Marc Robbins.

Trickery. Universal/Laemmle. Two reels. Screenplay: Clarence Badger and Frank Lloyd. With Frank Lloyd, Millard K. Wilson, Marc Robbins, Helen Leslie.

Their Golden Wedding. Universal/Laemmle. One reel. Screenplay: John Fleming Wilson. With Charles Manley, Mother Benson, Marc Robbins, Millard K. Wilson.

From the Shadows. Universal/Laemmle. One reel. Screenplay: Ben Cohn and Frank Lloyd. With Frank Lloyd, Marc Robbins, Helen Leslie.

Little Mr. Fixer. Universal/Laemmle. One reel. Screenplay: Frank Lloyd, based on a story by Maurice de la Parelle. With Millard K. Wilson, Olive Gordon, Marc Robbins.

Eleven to One. Universal/Laemmle. One reel. Screenplay: Harvey Gates. With Frank Lloyd, Marc Robbins, Peggy Hart.

Billie's Baby. Universal/Laemmle. One reel. Screenplay: George E. Jenks. With Peggy Hart, Millard K. Wilson, Marc Robbins.

Martin Lowe, Fixer. Universal/Laemmle. One reel. Screenplay: Ben Cohen and Frank Lloyd. With Frank Lloyd, Millard K. Wilson, Marc Robbins.

His Superior's Honor. Universal/Laemmle. One reel. Screenplay: Frank Lloyd. With Millard K. Wilson, Gretchen Lederer, Marc Robbins.

According to Value. Universal/Laemmle. One reel. Screenplay: Harvey Gates and Frank Lloyd. With Frank Lloyd, Millard K. Wilson, Gretchen Lederer.

Paternal Love. Universal/Laemmle. One reel. Screenplay: Frank Lloyd, based on a story by William Wolbert. With Millard K. Wilson, Gretchen Lederer, Marc Robbins.

The Source of Happiness. Universal/Laemmle. One reel. Screenplay: Louis V. Jefferson. With Charles Manley, Millard K. Wilson, Gretchen Lederer.

In the Grip of the Law. Universal/Laemmle. One reel. Screenplay: Frank Lloyd. With Millard K. Wilson, Olive Golden, Marc Robbins.

A Double Deal in Pork. Universal/Powers. One reel. Screenplay: Ruth Ann Baldwin and Rex de Roselli. With Marie Walcamp, Lule Warrenton, William Clifford.

Dr. Mason's Temptation. Universal/Laemmle. One reel. Screenplay: Frank Lloyd, based on a story by Hugh Weir. With Millard K. Wilson, Olive Golden, Marc Robbins.

The Gentleman from Indiana. Pallas/Paramount. Five reels. Based on the novel by Booth Tarkington. With Dustin Farnum, Winifred Kingston, Herbert Standing, Page Peters.

Jane. Oliver Morosco/Paramount. Five reels. Based on the play by W.H. Lestocq and Harry Nicholls. With Charlotte Greenwood, Sydney Grant, Myrtle Stedman, Forrest Stanley.

The Reform Candidate. Pallas/Paramount. Five reels. Screenplay: Maclyn Arbuckle and Edgar A. Guest. With Maclyn Arbuckle, Forrest Stanley, Myrtle Stedman.

1916

Tongues of Men. Oliver Morosco/Paramount. Five reels. Screenplay: Elliott J. Clawson, based on the play by Edward Childs. With Constance Collier, Forrest Stanley, Herbert Standing, Lamarr Johnstone.

Madame La Presidente. Oliver Morosco/Paramount. Five reels. Screenplay: Elliott J. Clawson, based on the play by Maurice Hennequin, Pierre Veber and Jose G. Levy. With Anna Held, Forrest Stanley, Herbert Standing, Page Peters.

The Code of Marcia Gray. Oliver Morosco/Paramount. Five reels. Screenplay: Frank Lloyd. With Constance Collier, Harry De Vere, Forrest Stanley, Herbert Standing.

David Garrick. Pallas/Paramount. Five reels. Based on the play by T.W. Robertson. With Dustin Farnum, Winifred Kingston, Herbert Standing.

The Making of Maddalena. Oliver Morosco/Paramount. Five reels. Screenplay: L.V. Jefferson, based on the play by Samuel G. Lewis and Mary E. Lewis. With Edna Goodrich, Forrest Stanley, Howard Davies.

An International Marriage. Oliver Morosco/Paramount. Five reels. Based on the play by George Broadhurst. With Rita Jolivet, Marc Robbins, Elliott Dexter, Grace Carlisle.

The Stronger Love. Oliver Morosco/Paramount. Screenplay: Alice von Saxmar. With Vivian Martin, Edward Peil, Frank Lloyd, Herbert Standing.

The Intrigue. Pallas/Paramount. Five reels. Screenplay: Julia Crawford Ivers. With Leonore Ulrich, Cecil Van Auker, Howard Davies, Florence Vidor.

Sins of Her Parent. Fox. Five reels. Screenplay: Frank Lloyd, based on a story by Thomas Forman. With Gladys Brockwell, William Clifford, Carl Von Schiller.

1917

The Price of Silence. Fox. Five reels. Screenplay: Frank Lloyd, based on a story by Mildred Pigott and William Pigott. With William Farnum, Frank Clark, Vivian Rich.

A Tale of Two Cities. Fox. Seven reels. Screenplay: Frank Lloyd, based on the novel by Charles Dickens. With William Farnum, Jewel Carmen, Charles Clary, Herschel Mayall.

American Methods. Fox. Five reels. Screenplay: F. McGrew Willis and Frank Lloyd, based on the novel, *Le Maitre de Forges*, by Georges Ohnet. With William Farnum, Jewel Carmen, Bertram Grassby, Willard Louis.

When a Man Sees Red. Fox. Five reels. Screenplay: Frank Lloyd, based on a short story by Larry Evans. With William Farnum, Jewel Carmen, G. Raymond Nye.

The Heart of a Lion. Fox. Five reels. Screenplay: Frank Lloyd, based on the novel, *The Doctor: A Tale of the Rockies*, by Ralph Connor. With William Farnum, Mary Martin, William Courtleigh, Jr.

1918

Les Miserables. Fox. Nine reels. Screenplay: Frank Lloyd and Marc Robbins, based on the novel by Victor Hugo. With William Farnum, George Moss, Sonia Markova, Jewel Carmen.

The Blindness of Divorce. Fox. Nine reels. Screenplay: Frank Lloyd. With Charles Clary, Rhea Mitchell, Bertram Grassby.

True Blue. Fox. Six reels. Screenplay: Frank Lloyd. With William Farnum, Frances Carpenter, Charles Clary, Katherine Adams.

Riders of the Purple Sage. Fox. Seven reels. Screenplay: Frank Lloyd, based on the novel by Zane Grey. With William Farnum, William Scott, Marc Robbins, Murdock MacQuarrie.

The Rainbow Trail. Fox. Six reels. Screenplay: Charles Kenyon and Frank Lloyd, based on the novel by Zane Grey. With William Farnum, Ann Forrest, Mary Mersch, Buck Jones.

[*William Farnum in a Liberty Loan Film*]. One reel. No director credit but assumed to be the work of Frank Lloyd.

For Freedom. Fox. Six reels. Screenplay: E. Lloyd Sheldon and Florence Margolies. With William Farnum. Ruby De Remer, Anna Lehr.

1919

The Man Hunter. Fox. Six reels. Screenplay: Frank Lloyd. With William Farnum, Louise Lovely, Charles Clary, Marc Robbins.

Pitfalls of a Big City. Fox. Five reels. Screenplay: Bennett R. Cohen. With Gladys Brockwell, William Scott, Neva Gerber.

The World and Its Woman. Goldwyn. Seven reels. Screenplay: Edward T. Lowe, Jr., based on a story by Thompson Buchanan. With Geraldine Farrar, Lou Tellegen, May Giraci, Alec B. Francis.

The Loves of Letty. Goldwyn. Five reels. Screenplay: J.E. Nash, based on the play, *Letty*, by Sir Arthur Wing Pinero. With Pauline Frederick, John Bowers, Lawson Butt, Willard Louis.

1920

The Woman in Room 13. Goldwyn. Five reels. Screenplay: E. Richard Schayer, based on the play by Samuel Shipman, Max Marcin and Percival Wilde. With Pauline Frederick, Charles Clary, John Bowers, Robert McKim.

The Silver Horde. Eminent Authors/Goldwyn. Six reels. Screenplay: Lawrence Trimble and J.E. Nash, based on the novel, *The Silver Horse*, by Rex Beach. With Myrtle Stedman, Curtis Cooksey, Betty Blythe, Robert McKim.

Madame X. Goldwyn. Seven reels. Screenplay: J.E. Nash and Frank Lloyd, based on the play, *La Femme X…*, by Alexandre Bisson. With Pauline Frederick, William Courtleigh, Hardee Kirkland, Casson Ferguson.

The Great Lover. Goldwyn. Six reels. Screenplay: J.E. Nash, based on the play by Leo Ditrichstein. With John Sainpolis, Claire Adams, John Davidson, Alice Hollister.

1921

A Tale of Two Worlds. Goldwyn. Six reels. Screenplay: J. Frank Glendon. With Leatrice Joy, Wallace Beery, Margaret McWade.

A Voice in the Dark. Goldwyn. Five reels. Screenplay: Arthur F. Statter, based on the play by Ralph E. Dyar. With Ramsey Wallace, Irene Rich, Alec Francis, Alan Hale.

Roads of Destiny. Goldwyn. Five reels. Screenplay: J.E. Nash, based on the play by Channing Pollock. With Pauline Frederick, John Bowers, Richard Tucker, Jane Novak.

The Invisible Power. Goldwyn. Seven reels. Screenplay: Charles Kenyon. With House Peters, Irene Rich, DeWitt Jennings, Sydney Ainsworth.

The Grim Comedian. Goldwyn. Six reels. Screenplay: Bess Meredyth, based on a story by Rita Weiman. With Phoebe Hunt, Jack Holt, Gloria Hope, Bert Woodruff.

The Man from Lost River. Goldwyn. Six reels. Screenplay: Lambert Hillyer and Arthur F. Statter, based on a story by Katharine Newlin Burt. With House Peters, Fritzi Brunette, Allan Forrest, James Gordon.

1922

The Eternal Flame. Norma Talmadge/Associated First National Pictures. Eight reels. Screenplay: Frances Marion, based on the novel, *La Duchesse de Langeais*, by Honoré Balzac. With Norma Talmadge, Adolphe Menjou, Wedgewood Nowell, Conway Tearle.

Oliver Twist. Jackie Coogan/Associated First National Pictures. Eight reels. Screenplay: Frank Lloyd and Harry Weil, based on the novel by Charles Dickens. With Jackie Coogan, Lon Chaney, Gladys Brockwell, George Siegmann.

The Sin Flood. Goldwyn. Seven reels. Screenplay: J.G.Hawks, based on the novel, *Syndafloden*, by Henning Berger. With Richard Dix, Helene Chadwick, James Kirkwood, Ralph Lewis.

1923

The Voice from the Minaret. Norma Talmadge/Associated First National Pictures. Seven reels. Screenplay: Frances Marion, based on the play by Robert Hichens. With Norma Talmadge, Eugene O'Brien, Edwin Stevens, Winter Hall.

Within the Law. Joseph Schenck/Associated First National Pictures. Eight reels. Screenplay: Frances Marion, based on the play by Bayard Veiller. With Norma Talmadge, Lew Cody, Jack Mulhall, Eileen Percy.

Ashes of Vengeance. Norma Talmadge/Associated First National Pictures. Ten reels. Screenplay: Frank Lloyd, based on the novel by H.B. Somerville. With Norma Talmadge, Conway Tearle, Wallace Beery, Josephine Crowell.

1924

Black Oxen. Frank Lloyd/Associated First National Pictures. Eight reels. Based on the novel by Gertrude Atherton. With Corinne Griffith, Conway Tearle, Thomas Ricketts, Clara Bow.

The Sea Hawk. Frank Lloyd/Associated First National Pictures. Twelve reels. Screenplay: J. G. Hawks, based on the novel by Rafael Sabatini. With Milton Sills, Enid Bennett, Lloyd Hughes, Wallace Beery, Wallace MacDonald.

The Silent Watcher. Frank Lloyd/Associated First National Pictures. Eight reels. Screenplay: J. G. Hawks. With Glenn Hunter, Bessie Love, Hobart Bosworth, Gertrude Astor.

1925

Her Husband's Secret. Frank Lloyd/Associated First National Pictures. Seven reels. Screenplay: J. G. Hawks, based on the story "Judgement" by May Edginton. With Antonio Moreno, Patsy Ruth Miller, Ruth Clifford, David Torrrence.

Winds of Chance. Frank Lloyd/Associated First National Pictures. Ten reels. Screenplay: J. G. Hawks, based on the novel by Rex Beach. With Anna Q. Nilsson, Ben Lyon, Viola Dana, Hobart Bosworth.

The Splendid Road. Frank Lloyd/Associated First National Pictures. Eight reels. Screenplay: J. G. Hawks, based on the novel by Vingie E. Roe. With Anna Q. Nilsson, Robert Frazer, Lionel Barrymore, DeWitt Jennings.

1926

The Wise Guy. Frank Lloyd/Associated First National Pictures. Eight reels. Screenplay: Ada McQuillin, George Marion, Jr. and Adela Rogers St. Johns, based on a story by Jules Furthman. With Mary Astor, James Kirkwood, Betty Compson, George F. Marion.

The Eagle of the Sea. Famous Players-Lasky/Paramount. Eight reels. Screenplay: Julien Josephson, based on the novel, *Captain Sazarac*, by Charles Tenney Jackson. With Florence Vidor, Ricardo Cortez, Sam De Grasse, André Beranger.

1927

Children of Divorce. Famous Players-Lasky/Paramount. Seven reels. Screenplay: Hope Loring and Louis D. Lighton, based on the novel by Owen Johnson. With Clara Bow, Esther Ralston, Gary Cooper, Einar Hanson.

1928

Adoration. First National Pictures. Seven reels. Screenplay: Winifred Dunn, based on a story by Lajos Biró. With Billie Dove, Antonio Moreno, Emile Chautard, Lucy Dorraine.

1929

Weary River. First National Pictures. Eight reels. Screenplay: Bradley King. With Richard Barthelmess, Betty Compson, William Holden, Louis Natheaux. Released in both silent and sound versions.

The Divine Lady. First National Pictures. Twelve reels. Screenplay: Agnes Christine Johnson, based on the novel by E. Barrington. With Corinne Griffith, Victor Varconi, H.B. Warner, Marie Dressler. Released with music and sound effects.

Drag. First National Pictures. Nine reels. Screenplay: Bradley King, based on the play by William Dudley Pelley. With Richard Barthelmess, Lucien Littlefield, Katherine Ward, Alice Day. Released in both silent and sound versions.

Dark Streets. First National Pictures. Six reels. Screenplay: Bradley King. With Jack Mulhall, Lila Lee, Aggie Herring, Earl Pingree.

Young Nowheres. First National Pictures. Seven reels. Screenplay: Bradley King, based on the story by Ida Alexa Ross Wylie. With Richard Barthelmess, Marion Nixon, Bert Roach, Anders Randolf. Released in both silent and sound versions.

1930

Son of the Gods. First National Pictures. Nine reels. Screenplay: Bradley King, based on the story by Rex Beach. With Richard Barthelmess, Constance Bennett, Dorothy Mathews, Barbara Leonard. Released in both silent and sound versions.

The Way of All Men. First National Pictures. Seven reels. Screenplay: Bradley King, based on the novel, *Syndafloden*, by Henning Berger. With Douglas Fairbanks, Jr., Dorothy Revier, Robert Edeson, Anders Randolf.

The Lash. First National Pictures. Nine reels. Screenplay: Bradley King, based on the novel, *Adiós!*, by Lanier Bartlett and Virginia Stivers. With Richard Barthelmess, Mary Astor, Fred Kohler, Marion Nixon. Shot in widescreen (Vitascope) 65mm.

1931

The Right of Way. First National Pictures. 75 mins. Screenplay: Francis Edward Faragoh, based on the novel by Sir Gilbert Parker. With Conrad Nagel, Loretta Young, Fred Kohler, William Janney.

East Lynne. Fox. 104 mins. Screenplay: Bradley King and Tom Barry, based on the novel by Mrs. Henry Wood. With Ann Harding, Clive Brook, Conrad Nagel, Cecelia Loftus Beryl Mercer.

The Age for Love. Caddo Co./United Artists. 81 mins. Screenplay: Ernest Pascal and Frank Lloyd, based on the novel by Ernest Pascal. With Billie Dove, Charles Starrett, Lois Wilson, Edward Everett Horton. Frank Lloyd also produced.

1932

A Passport to Hell. Fox. 75 mins. Screenplay: Bradley King and Leon Gordon, based on an unpublished novel by Harry Hervey. With Elissa Landi, Paul Lukas, Warner Oland, Donald Crisp.

1933

Cavalcade. Fox. 110 mins. Screenplay: Reginald Berkeley and Sonya Levien, based on the play by Noel Coward. With Diana Wynyard, Clive Brook, Una O'Connor, Frank Lawton.

Berkeley Square. Fox. 90 mins. Screenplay: Sonya Levien and John L. Balderston, based on the play by John L. Balderston and J.C. Squire. With Leslie Howard, Heather Angel, Valerie Taylor, Irene Browne.

Hoop-La. Fox. 85 mins. Screenplay: Bradley King and Joseph Moncure March, based on the play, *The Barker*, by John Kenyon Nicholson. With Clara Bow, Preston Foster, Richard Cromwell, Herbert Mundin.

1934

Servants' Entrance. Fox. 90 mins. Screenplay: Samson Raphaelson, based on the novel, *Vi som gar kjøkkenveien*, by Sigrid Boo. With Janet Gaynor, Lew Ayres, Ned Sparks, Walter Connolly.

1935

Mutiny on the Bounty. Metro-Goldwyn-Mayer. 132 mins. Screenplay: Talbot Jennings, Jules Furthman and Carey Wilson, based on the novel by Charles Nordhoff and James Norman Hall and their novel, *Men Against the Sea*. With Charles Laughton, Clark Gable, Franchot Tone, Herbert Mundin. Frank Lloyd also co-produced with Irving Thalberg. Reissued in 1939.

1936

Under Two Flags. 20th Century-Fox. 111 mins. Screenplay: W.P. Lipscomb and Walter Ferris, based on the novel by Ouida. With Ronald Colman, Claudette Colbert, Victor McLaglen, Rosalind Russell.

1937

Maid of Salem. Paramount. 86 mins. Screenplay: Walter Ferris, Bradley King and Durward Grinstead, based on a story by Bradley King. With Claudette Colbert, Fred MacMurray, Harvey Stephens, Gale Sondergaard.

Wells Fargo. Paramount. 115 mins. Screenplay: Paul Schofield, Gerald Geraghty and Frederick Jackson, based on a story by Stuart N. Lake. With Joel McCrea, Bob Burns, Frances Dee, Lloyd Nolan. Reissued in 1958 on a double bill with *The Forest Rangers*.

1938

If I Were King. Paramount. 100 mins. Screenplay: Preston Sturges, based on the play by Justin Huntly McCarthy. With Ronald Colman, Basil Rathbone, Frances Dee, Henry Wilcoxon.

1939

Rulers of the Sea. Paramount. 96 mins. Screenplay: Talbot Jennings, Frank Cavett and Richard Collins. With Douglas Fairbanks, Jr., Margaret Lockwood, Will Fyffe, George Bancroft.

1940

The Howards of Virginia. Frank Lloyd Pictures/Columbia. 122 mins. Screenplay: Sidney Buchman, based on the novel, *The Tree of Liberty*, by Elizabeth Page. With Cary Grant, Martha Scott, Cedric Hardwicke, Alan Marshall. Frank Lloyd also produced.

1941

The Lady from Cheyenne. Frank Lloyd Productions/Universal. 87 mins. Screenplay: Warren Duff and Kathryn Scola, based on a story by Jonathan Finn and Theresa Oaks. With Loretta Young, Robert Preston, Edward Arnold, Frank Craven. Frank Lloyd also produced.

This Woman Is Mine. Frank Lloyd Productions/Universal. 92 mins. Screenplay: Seton I. Miller and Frederick Jackson, based on the novel, *I, James Lewis*, by Gilbert Wolf Gabriel. With Franchot Tone, John Carroll, Walter Brennan, Carol Bruce. Frank Lloyd also produced.

1942

Saboteur. Frank Lloyd Productions/Universal. 108 mins. Director: Alfred Hitchcock. Screenplay: Peter Viertel, Joan Harrison and Dorothy Parker. With Priscilla Lane, Robert Cummings, Otto Kruger, Norman Lloyd. Produced but not directed by Frank Lloyd.

The Spoilers. Frank Lloyd Productions/Universal. 87 mins. Director: Ray Enright. Screenplay: Lawrence Hazard and Tom Reed, based on the novel by Rex Beach. With Marlene Dietrich, Randolph Scott, John Wayne, Margaret Lindsay. Produced but not directed by Frank Lloyd.

The Invisible Agent. Universal. 79 mins. Director: Edwin L. Marin. Screenplay: Curt Siodmak. With Ilona Massey, Jon Hall, Cedric Hardwicke, J. Edward Bromberg. Produced but not directed by Frank Lloyd.

1943

Forever and a Day. Anglo-American Film Co./RKO. 105 mins. Frank Lloyd is one of the seven directors credited on the film, along with 21 screenwriters. According to *The Hollywood Reporter* (September 21, 1942), Lloyd directed the London blitz sequences with which the production opens and closes.

1944
Air Pattern – Pacific. U.S. Army/Office of War Information. 42 mins. Documentary.

1945
Blood on the Sun. Cagney Productions/United Artists. 98 mins. Screenplay: Lester Cole, based on a story by Garrett Fort and an idea by Frank Melford. With James Cagney, Sylvia Sidney, Porter Hall, John Emery.

1946
The Last Bomb. Warner Bros. 18 mins. Documentary.

1954
The Shanghai Story. Republic. 90 mins. Screenplay: Seton I. Miller and Steve Fisher, based on a story by Lester Yard. With Ruth Roman, Edmond O'Brien, Richard Jaeckel, Whit Bissell. Frank Lloyd also produced.

1955
The Last Command. Republic. 110 mins. Screenplay: Warren Duff, based on a story by Sy Bartlett. With Sterling Hayden, Anna Maria Alberghetti, Richard Carlson, Ernest Borgnine. Frank Lloyd also produced.

INDEX

Academy Awards 10, 98, 111, 142, 150, 151
Academy of Motion Picture Arts and
  Sciences 11
The Age for Love 77
Air Pattern – Pacific 138
Angel, Heather 81, 96
As the Wind Blows 20
Ashes of Vengeance 47
Astor, Mary 77
Atherton, Gertrude 56
Ayes, Lew 138, 150
Balderston, John L. 96, 99
Barnes, Binnie 89
Barrymore, John 71
Barthelmess, Richard 72-77
Beery, Wallace 39, 49, 52
Bennett, Enid 50, 51
Berkeley, Reginald 90, 93
Berkeley Square 82, 96
The Black Box 18
The Black Oxen 56-58
Blood on the Sun 13, 139-142
Borgnine, Ernest 9, 148
Borzage, Frank 87, 98, 150
Bow, Clara 10, 56, 58, 70
Brook, Clive 81, 83, 84, 85, 89, 93
Brockwell, Gladys 29, 40
Brower, Otto 117
Browne, Irene 82, 89, 96
Bruce, Nigel 135
The Buccaneers 48
Cagney, James 139, 140
Capra, Frank 95, 150
Captain Kidd 48, 161
Carmen, Jewel 31, 32
Carroll, Leo G. 135
Catalina Island 49, 59, 105
Cavalcade 10, 12, 13, 26, 81, 86-95
Chaney, Lon 40

The Children of Divorce 58, 69-71
Churchill, Frank 74
Circle 17 18
The Code of Marcia Gray 25
Cohn, Harry 127
Colbert, Claudette 10, 123, 124, 135
Collier, Constance 25
Colman, Ronald 10, 81, 117, 120, 121
The Come-Back 22
Coogan, Jackie 10, 40, 41, 42
Cooke, Alistair 127
Cooper, Gary 70, 71, 150
Cortez, Ricardo 55
Coward, Noel 86, 87, 90
Damon and Pythias 19
Dangers of the Veldt 18
David Garrick 23-25, 26
The Dead Line 18
Dee, Frances 125
Delfino, Joseph 48
DeMille, Cecil B. 9, 64, 135
Dickens, Charles 11, 12, 29, 30-32, 40, 41,
  42, 43
The Divine Lady 10, 14, 58-66
Dr. Mason's Temptation 22
Dove, Billie 77
Drag 75
Dressler, Marie 60, 62-63
The Eagle of the Sea 55-56
East Lynne 77, 82-86
Estabrook, Howard 125
Fairbanks, Jr., Douglas 112
Farnum, Dustin 23-25, 136
Farnum, William 29-35, 136
Farrar, Geraldine 37, 48
The Flying Yorkshireman 133
For Freedom 32
For the Freedom of Cuba 18
Forever and a Day 137

Foster, Billy 31
Fox, William 29, 34, 35, 36
Frank Lloyd Pictures, Inc. 133
Frank Lloyd Productions Pictures, Inc. 129, 133
From the Shadows 22
Fyffe, Will 81, 112
Gable, Clark 10, 103, 106, 109, 111
Genesis IV – 9 17
The Gentleman from Indiana 23, 26
Goldwyn Pictures Corporation 36, 38
Grant, Cary 10, 129, 150
Granville, Bonita 123
Gray, Franklin 145
Greenwood, Charlotte 25
Grey, Zane 34, 35
Griffith, Corinne 10, 26, 56-66
Hageman, Richard 112
Hall, James Norman 103-104
Haller, Alma 15, 145
Harding, Ann 83, 85
Hartford, David 48
Hayden, Sterling 147, 148
Held, Anna 25
Her Husband's Secret 55
His Captive 18
His Last Serenade 18
Hitchcock, Alfred 136
Hoop-La 58, 81
Howard, Leslie 10, 81, 96, 98
The Howards of Virginia 10, 26, 127-129
Hughes, Lloyd 49-50, 51, 54
Hugo, Victor 11, 32, 33
Hunnicutt, Arthur 147
If I Were King 120-123, 145
Ingram, Rex 51
The Invisible Agent 135-136
Jackson, Charles Tenney 55
James, Henry 96
Jane 25
Jennings, Talbot 105, 112
Joy, Leatrice 39
Kellogg, Virginia 149-150
King, Bradley 72, 86, 124
Knight, Eric 133
The Lady from Cheyenne 133, 145
Landi, Elissa 86
Larkin, George 20
The Lash 77

The Last Bomb 139
The Last Command 9, 147-150
Laughton, Charles 10, 12, 81, 103, 109, 110, 111, 114, 150
The Law of the Land 18
Leslie, Helen 20
Lewis and Lake Company 15
Lockwood, Margaret 81, 112
Loftus, Cecelia 83
London 14
MacMurray, Fred 123
Madame La Presidente 25
Madame X 11-12, 37-38
The Madonna of the Slums 18
Maid of Salem 123-125
Martin, Vivian 25
Martin Lowe, Financier 18
Mayfair Productions 133
McCrea, Joel 60, 125, 126, 150
Mercer, Beryl 81, 84, 85
Miller, Don 48
Mills, John 89
Les Miserables 32-34
Movietone City 90
Mundin, Herbert 81, 94, 103
Murray, Johnny 74
Mutiny on the Bounty 10, 12, 14, 81, 103-112, 114
Nagel, Conrad 83, 84
Nordhoff, Charles 103-104
Nature's Triumph 18
Nixon, Marion 75, 77
Oboler, Arch 133
O'Connor, Una 81, 89, 94
Oliver Morosco Company 23-25
Oliver Twist 12-13, 40-43, 151-152
On the Rio Grande 18
Pallas Pictures, Inc. 23-25
Papa Married a Mormon 149
Parish, Robert 60-61
Parsons, Louella 58, 124, 128, 141, 145
Passport to Hell 86
Preston, Robert 134
The Price of Silence 29
A Prince of Bavaria 19
Prisco, Albert 54
Prowlers of the Wild 18
The Rainbow Trail 35
Ralston, Esther 70

Reiter, William J.   48
Republic Pictures   146-149
Riders of the Purple Sage   34, 35
Roach, Bert   76
Robbins, Marc   20
Rogers, Will   94, 95
Royal Rogue   20
Rulers of the Sea   9, 14, 112-114
Sabatini, Rafael   51, 55
Saboteur   135-136
Schenck, Joseph M.   47, 71, 150
Scotland   10, 14, 151-152
Scott, Martha   129
The Sea Hawk   10, 12, 14, 48-55
The Sea Squawk   55
The Shanghai Story   146-147
Sidney, Sylvia   139
The Silent Watcher   55
Sills, Milton   10, 49, 50-51, 54
The Silver Horde   36
Simon, Simone   117-118
The Sin Flood   39-40
Sins of Her Parents   29
Skirball, Jack   136-137
Son of the Gods   76-77
The Splendid Road   55
The Spoilers   135-136
Stedman, Myrtle   36
Sterling, Jack   137
The Stronger Love   25
Sturges, Preston   122
A Tale of Two Cities   30-32
A Tale of Two Worlds   39
Talmadge, Norma   47
Taylor, Valerie   82, 96
Tempest   71
The Temptation of Edwin Swayne   18
That Hamilton Woman   66
This Woman Is Mine   134-135, 145
Through the Flames   18
Tinker, Edward Richmond   87
Tone, Franchot   103, 107, 111, 134
Tongues of Men   25
Tottenham, Merle   89, 94
Traffic in Babies   19
Trevor, Norman   60
Turner, Otis   19-20, 21
Twitchell, Waldo   112
Under Two Flags   81, 117-120

Universal   17-22
The Vagabond   20
Varconi, Victor   59, 60, 64-65
Vidor, Florence   55
Waggner, George   136
Walker Theatrical Enterprises   15
Warner, H.B.   60, 64
Weary River   72-74
Weber, Lois   17, 19
Wells Fargo   9, 10, 26, 125-127, 128, 137
Westmore, Ernest   49
Wilson, Millard K.   22
Winds of Chance   55
Witney, William   148
The Woman in Black   18
Won in the Clouds   161
Wood, Mrs. Henry   82
The World and Its Woman   36-37
Wynyard, Diana   13, 81, 84, 89, 93
Young, Loretta   10, 133, 134
Young Nowheres   75-76
Zanuck, Darryl F.   118, 119

ABOUT THE AUTHOR

Rightly described as a "one-man publishing phenomenon" by the Los Angeles *Times*, Anthony Slide is the author of more than seventy books on the history of popular entertainment and editor of a further 150 volumes. He published his first book, *Early American Cinema*, in 1970, and since then he has written many other pioneering works including *Early Women Directors* (1977, revised and rewritten as *The Silent Feminists*, 1996), *Great Pretenders: A History of Female and Male Impersonation in the Performing Arts* (1986), *The Cinema and Ireland* (1988), *Nitrate Won't Wait: A History of Film Preservation in the United States* (1992), *Before Video: A History of the Non-Theatrical Film* (1992), and *Lois Weber: The Director Who Lost Her Way in History* (1996). Two of his books, *The American Film Industry: A Historical Dictionary* (1986) and *The Encyclopedia of Vaudeville* (1994) have been named Outstanding Reference Source of the Year by the American Library Association.

Among his more recent works are *Silent Players: A Biographical and Autobiographical Study of 100 Silent Film Actors and Actresses* (2002), *American Racist: The Life and Films of Thomas Dixon* (2004) and *Now Playing: Hand-Painted Poster Art from the 1910s through the 1950s* (2007). In 2007, BearManor Media published Slide's *Incorrect Entertainment, or, Trash from the Past: A History of Political Inccorectness and Bad Taste in 20th Century American Popular Culture.*

A world-renowned historian, Anthony Slide has served as associate archivist of the American Film Institute and resident film historian of the Academy of Motion Picture Arts and Sciences. He has produced a number of documentaries on silent film personalities, including the feature-length *The Silent Feminists: America's First Women Directors*; served as a consultant or participant on many television programs and documentaries; and also contributed a number of DVD commentaries for 20th Century Fox and Warner Bros. For more information on his activities, readers are invited to check out his website at anthonyslide.com and his regular commentary on film books at *theslidearea.com*.

www.ingramcontent.com/pod-product-compliance
Lightning Source LLC
Chambersburg PA
CBHW050803160426
43192CB00010B/1625